KING OF THE GOLD COAST

KING OF THE GOLD COAST

CAP'N STREETER, THE MILLIONAIRES
AND THE STORY OF
LAKE SHORE DRIVE

WAYNE KLATT

Charleston   London

THE
History
PRESS

Published by The History Press
Charleston, SC 29403
www.historypress.net

Cover design and illustrations by Karleigh Hambrick.

First published 2011

Manufactured in the United States

ISBN 978.1.60949.320.2

Library of Congress Cataloging-in-Publication Data

Klatt, Wayne.
King of the Gold Coast : Cap'n Streeter, the millionaires and the story of Lake Shore Drive
/ Wayne Klatt.
p. cm.
Includes bibliographical references.
ISBN 978-1-60949-320-2
1. Streeter, George Wellington, 1837-1921. 2. Chicago (Ill.)--Biography. 3. Chicago (Ill.)--
History--1875- 4. Gold Coast (Chicago, Ill.) 5. Lake Shore Drive (Chicago, Ill.)--History. I.
Title.
F548.45.S87K53 2011
977.3'041092--dc23
[B]
2011020366

What is the city but the people?
–Coriolanus, *Act II, scene 1*

CONTENTS

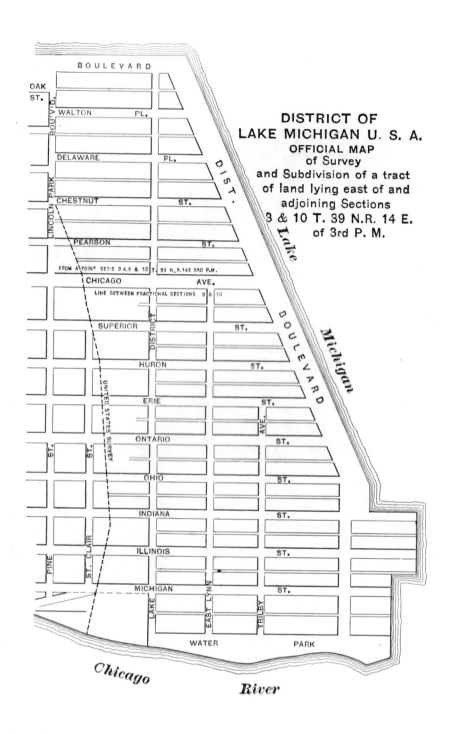

Streeter's bogus map of the District of Lake Michigan, showing imaginary streets and calling Lake Shore Drive "District Boulevard." *Captain Streeter Pioneer.*

INTRODUCTION

In early 1885, a lacquered carriage rolled onto the wasteland a mile north of Chicago's business district and stopped at a newly completed sandstone and granite mansion. The city's most prominent businessman, Potter Palmer, and his stylish wife, Bertha, stepped down and for the first time entered their million-dollar castellated home, the largest in the city. The building was so exclusive that its exterior doors had no keyholes, so that they could be opened only from within by servants.[1] There were no neighbors to greet them, no sign of life but frogs and rabbits and no sounds but the lapping of Lake Michigan upon the lonely shore.

Palmer's quiet boldness in moving to this marsh was only the opening gambit in transforming affluent living in the city. Out of this would evolve not just the elite Lake Shore Drive residential district but also the "Magnificent Mile" of trendy shops along North Michigan Avenue and the city's miles of public beaches. Yet the story of how this plan came to life has never been told before.

That we know anything about the machinations is partly because of a born loser named George Wellington Streeter. With little more than bravado, a shotgun and a presidential forgery, he claimed responsibility for all 186 acres of the city's Gold Coast, and for years he made a livelihood selling deeds to property he never owned.

Streeter and Palmer: could two men ever be more dissimilar? Streeter enjoyed making himself cartoonish, telling tall tales of daring and living

Potter Palmer, the quiet man who
reshaped Chicago. *Chicago History
Museum.*

off promises and credit. But the immensely wealthy Palmer conducted
his life like the poker player he was, keeping most thoughts to himself.

Although not a financier, the prematurely gray and rather good-looking
man possessed one of the keenest business minds in the country. He let
his wife host lavish parties and clutter the interior of their castle with
drapes and ostrich feathers, but Palmer preferred keeping to his simple
tower bedroom, where he could relax and think things through at the end
of the day. At times he must have looked across the lake with its many
moods and brilliant sunrises and reminisced about his first love: baseball.

The sixteen-year culture clash created by these two men involved
prosperous merchants, the homeless, working-class investors and several
scoundrels. The results were a class war, a war of nerves and eventually
a shooting war that ended with Streeter being sentenced to life in prison.
After being freed on a technicality, he gleefully went on with his land
swindles even though fewer people believed him. In time he, himself, was
among them.

Previous accounts about Streeter and Lake Shore Drive have been
radically in error. This is the only work that uses primary sources and a

broad range of other material to navigate between the lies and silences on both sides. The story that emerges is one of a magnificent land grab that has incalculably benefitted the city, as well as charities and respected institutions.

THE INCONSTANT SHORE

To understand the conversion of worthless land into real estate gold, you need to know the conditions before Streeter arrived.

As a result of continual erosion at the southern dip of the Great Lakes, city officials were never sure where Chicago ended and the rest of the world began. The eastern edge of downtown had been filled in with rubble from the great fire of 1871, but the area north of the river was left a wilderness of dunes and scrub land that turned to swamp with every hard rain. A city pier built to accommodate lumber ships and steamboats accelerated the washing away of the sandy shore, forcing Chicago to grow ever southward.[2]

This did not stop the city from becoming the wonder and symbol of the age. For although the Mississippi separates east from west, Chicago joined the two by being on a water route from Canada to the Gulf of Mexico. In time it also became the railroad hub of America. Since this was the transfer point for twenty-six railways at six passenger terminals, to go by rail from one region to another usually meant a layover of a few hours or a day in the midst of charlatans, gamblers and dreamers.[3]

All politics and important business was conducted downtown or in a scattering of mansions and stylish restaurants on the South and West Sides. Only a few middle-class families, most of them German, moved north of the river to escape downtown congestion and the stench of the infamous South Side stockyards. Even then, erosion kept their homes inland for the equivalent of several blocks.

We have only one glimpse of what was on Palmer's mind when he thought about revolutionizing the ignored northern shore. In a sketchy account written years after the conversation, Palmer looked away from his friends and calmly mentioned, "I'm going there, north, to work out a new residence district."[4] What, build homes of stone upon sand?

"It will sink into the lake," one of his friends said. He should have remembered that Palmer never—ever—made an unwise business decision.

Anyone could have conceived a simple residential development plan, but no one else in the city had the vision and influence to pull it off. As proof, John Jacob Astor once owned the general area but did nothing with it, and his estate gladly sold off the lots cheaply and piecemeal. The Roman Catholic archdiocese purchased half a mile bordering the wilderness for its headquarters and a graveyard, but the cemetery had to be abandoned because of the encroaching lake.

The shape of the marsh was so uncertain that maps classified it as "property open to entry," a haven for transients and occasional squatters. After a downpour, people who had bought any portion in the hope that something worthwhile might be built nearby would row out to see if their vacant lots were still there.

"The shore warn't nothin' but an ol' dump for garbage and dead cats," Streeter would say.[5] You could walk across it without ever seeing a fence or warning sign.

The Plan

Everything that followed stemmed from the way the state legislature rather than the city controlled the shore. Since the city had been too busy growing to concern itself with planning, the state created the Lincoln Park Board in 1864 to improve the unwieldy north end of the long, narrow marsh by imposing a special tax on residents in Chicago's North Township and on people living in what was then the adjacent town of Lake View.[6] With winds and lake currents making landscaping impossible, the commissioners solidified the shore with a landscaped carriageway over buried waste material.[7]

Although no one had determined whether property below water belonged to the federal government or the state, the Illinois General Assembly authorized the park commissioners to defray construction costs by selling deeds to submerged lands within their taxing area "in fee simple" (absolute ownership).[8]

Because of this, the carriageway began a little outside the park, at the end of what was then Pine Street (North Michigan Avenue). The carriageway began as Pine Street Drive but turned into Lake Shore Drive inside the park, where it circled around a flower garden. The handsome boulevard primarily offered affluent families a refreshing buggy ride on lazy Sunday afternoons.

Palmer lived in his famed downtown hotel, the Palmer House, but a number of other prominent civic leaders had mansions at Eighteenth Street and Prairie Avenue, two miles south of downtown. British reformer William Stead wrote after seeing Prairie Avenue that "probably there are as many millions of dollars to the square inch of this residence district as are to be found in any equal on the world's surface."[9] Yet in perhaps no other city did its wealthy live so close to a red-light district and have such smoky air.

New mansions were soon aged by a constant swathing of soot from trains along the other side of a brick wall, and the befouled air was blamed for health problems from sniffles to pneumonia. But Prairie Avenue families did not want to relocate to the west or farther south because middle- and working-class housing would hem them in. Besides, that would bring them closer to the stockyards and away from summer breezes off the lake.

And so to Palmer, in the north marsh lay the future. He had accomplished something like this once before, when the city's business district was cramped along east-running Lake Street, which led to the river mouth and harbor. Shop patrons shared wooden sidewalks with river men, and carriages were often snarled in traffic tangles with beer carts and furniture wagons.

Being an entrepreneur rather than a politician, Palmer approached the problem as a commercial venture. Just months after the great fire, he bought up a mile stretch of north-running State Road for about $1 million and donated half the frontage to the city with the understanding that it would be paved as Chicago's widest commercial avenue.

Next he anchored his portion of the renamed State Street with his hotel and the Field, Palmer & Leiter department store, later to become Marshall Field & Company and now a Macy's. Then he leased the rest of his side of the street to other stores. Rather than being merely a row of shops, State Street—"that great street" in song—became the heart of the Loop, the city's tight concentration of business, government, shopping and entertainment venues.

Seeing landfill being used for the Lincoln Park shoreline in the mid-1870s inspired a scattering of small-time investors and businesses to shelter their portion of the wasteland with refuse and sludge. As the aggressive Chicago Canal and Dock Company, run by the Ogdens, deepened the river mouth for the city's harbor, it used the mud to build its own miniharbor, called the (Lake) Michigan Canal and later the Ogden Slip. The enterprise helped make Chicago the busiest port in the country, with eleven million tons of cargo sailing in and out each year, even though many of the boats were aging lumber schooners.[10]

Palmer's land scheme would involve much more than just having a street built on dumpings. After all, his career was based on an ability to find solutions outside traditional thinking. The former Quaker had given up store clerking in upstate New York to strike out on his own at age seventeen and decided in his travels that more opportunities could be found in muddy Chicago than ore-rich California, if only because few others thought so.

Around 1882, he saw no reason why wealthy investors could not create an exclusive residential district just as the dock company had built its private harbor. But the concept did not arrive full-blown. From a brief newspaper mention, it seems that German immigrant Tobias Allmendinger, who had shielded his portion of empty shore with landfill near Oak Street, made a suggestion along these lines to the president of one of the smaller dredging companies, Charles Fitz-Simons.[11]

Unlike Palmer and his friends, the moderately tall, fashionably heavy Fitz-Simons was immediately approachable. His office was near the Michigan Canal/Ogden Slip, and he was often seen ambling about and acting important. This seemingly inconsequential fact would become important in the Streeterville saga.

The marine engineer had mastered dredging and bridge building in the Union army. He was intelligent by nature and a fool by choice. Fond of uniforms, the former general commanded a National Guard unit and loudly spoke his opinions no matter how wrong they were. Conveniently, he also was not above a little larceny.

Allmendinger may have only recommended constructing a seawall to protect the roughly three-quarters of a mile of wasteland that remained after Lincoln Park was completed. Whatever the idea was, Fitz-Simons evidently brought it up with Palmer. One of these three men—Allmendinger, Fitz-Simons or Palmer—came up with persuading the park board to extend its Lake Shore Drive all the way across the watery fringe of marsh.

Like all eminent entrepreneurs, Palmer could see needs changing a generation away, and now he envisioned the carriageway as the start of a carefully controlled metamorphosis in sumptuous homes. A major obstruction would be public attitude. In this bungalow metropolis, a stigma was still attached to sharing a building with another family. Only immigrants and factory workers were satisfied with apartments.

Palmer decided to reverse public preferences gradually, even if it took thirty years. To start the scheme, someone of prominence would have to relocate to the shore. Since this would mean a gamble and social

Palmer's "castle" on the marsh as it looked around 1900, after the shoreline was expanded, filled in and landscaped. *Author's collection.*

isolation, he would not call upon anyone to do it but himself. Once the park board went along with his vision, Palmer ordered that his landfill consist of nothing but unplowed black earth—from digging a Lincoln Park pond—and sand newly scooped from the lake. Once he moved to the wilderness, he began handpicking the next residents.

His spirit coincided with that of Chicago architect John Wellborn Root:

> *In America we are free of artistic traditions...We do shocking things... We try crude experiments...Yet somewhere in this mass of ungoverned energies lies the principal of life. A new spirit of beauty is being developed and perfected...This is not the same old thing made over; it is new.*[12]

Palmer had not been visualizing another Prairie Avenue district, where a few blocks of mansions with massive stone walls had no boulevard or commercial avenue to serve them. An architectural revolution was inevitable in the world's first skyscraper city, and he was certain that up-and-comers would want to be modern.

The latest residential craze among well-heeled New Yorkers was luxury apartments with all the amenities of a manor house, including servant's quarters, but without the cavernous waste and froufrou enjoyed by their fathers.

Chicago was expanding too rapidly and haphazardly for this conversion to happen without manipulation and guidance. Palmer had no personal desire to live on the marsh, and only his closest friends knew the real reason why he and his wife decided to move.

To stave off rival development, he kept his name and those of his venture partners out of any discussions of shore conversion beyond his "castle." A crucial element was persuading the Lincoln Park Board to build a landfill carriageway across marsh and water. As with any successful Chicago project of the day, this no doubt involved encouraging individual members with money or property. Although there is no proof of this, the air was thick with suspicion.

For convenience we say that Palmer did this and Palmer did that, but in reality, he was acting as head of an investors' syndicate involving an unknown number of local and out-of-town speculators.[13] The syndicate bought vacant marsh lots and granted ninety-nine-year leases to people who then subleased them for individual homes. The millionaires knew they must protect their investments by doing nothing that would give the plan away. This is as much as we can glean from what must have been lengthy and intricate private discussions.

Palmer chose the initial investors from among his friends at the Iroquois Club, which occupied the entire third floor of the downtown Columbia Theater building.[14] The wealthy Democrats enjoyed playing penny ante poker and discussing long-term business and civic goals among themselves. One of the players was Nathaniel Kellogg Fairbank, a soap manufacturer as well as the city's cultural leader. Another was John V. Farwell, who among his speculations held a share in sprawling Texas ranchland that would become the city of Austin.[15] But of all the Iroquois Club members, only Palmer would ever live on the marsh, and Farwell was the only one who had previously owned a piece of it. But the merchant became so disgusted with erosion that he sold his deed to the park board for a few dollars.

Internationally known portrait artist George P.A. Healy, who lived on the South Side, loved to tell the story of what happened when he accepted a deed to a patch of the marsh as payment for a painting in 1881. When he took the deed for Block 1 to the County Building, a clerk asked, "Do you really want this recorded?"

"Of course."

"But Mr. Healy, it will cost you five dollars."

"I know that, that is the usual amount, isn't it?"

"Yes, but, you see, Mr. Healy, this land is under the lake!"

Healy had the deed recorded anyway and later would sublease several lots in "Palmer's Addition to Chicago"—that is, in his landfill.[16]

Palmer, Farwell and Fairbank had already secured for their descendants a comfortable living as long as the stock market remained favorable. Either from the beginning or some time later, they decided to place much of the money that would be coming in from buildings on the "made land" into charitable trusts so that their favorite institutions would never have to scrape for funds again.

Evidently Palmer had in mind a true Gold Coast, a high-rent grid comprising Lake Shore Drive, Pine Street refashioned into a boulevard, and cross streets connecting the two thoroughfares. The genius of his concept was having individual mansions built only in the first phase. In time they would be flanked by apartment towers and then be torn down as society clamored for more high-rise living.

The planning occurred approximately between 1882 and 1884, a time when hidden land trusts, later to be called "Illinois trusts," were an untested idea being talked over amid cigar smoke in Chicago bank and real estate offices.[17] Without a legal means of keeping their names off documents once Palmer's castle was built, the parties needed subterfuge to prevent raids by investment pirates.

After Farwell and the Newberry family of businessmen and land speculators bought lots under Palmer's plan, they built small piers to make it look as if that was all they had sought the land for. Both little piers apparently went unused.

But Palmer had to act quickly. Just inland from the marsh, crews were starting to build the St. Benedict Flats apartment building at State Street and Chicago Avenue for the upper middle class. A rival developer mulling this over could easily start a lakeshore plan of his own.

And so no doubt Fitz-Simons appeared at Lincoln Park Board meetings, as later alleged by the Illinois attorney's office. The members accepted him as the general contractor without advertising for bids, in violation of a city law passed the year of the great fire. Evidence also suggests that the commissioners were encouraged to keep the plan from public disclosure, even though building the Drive well beyond the park would be the greatest Chicago public works project since the fire-ravaged city rebuilt itself.[18]

NOTE TO THE READER

Although the street now runs most of the city's length, Lake Shore Drive as used in this book refers only to the original stretch from Lincoln Park to just short of the Chicago River.

Out of necessity, several assumptions were needed for the events to make sense. As Victor Hugo said, "In all facts there are wheels within wheels."[19] The facts alone do not explain why judges made surprising decisions, an acting mayor sharply reversed himself in less than an hour and investigations were conducted only to end without calling for action. All assumptions are marked and explained in the notes section.

A few other things about this book call for clarification. The landowners have left us no account of their speculation, leaving us to watch the evolution of the marsh partly through Streeter's perspective. The two longest accounts of his fight with the millionaires, the putative biography *Captain Streeter Pioneer* and a portion of *Casebook of the Curious and True*, were written years after the incidents occurred. In wanting to improve the anecdotes, Streeter mythified them by mixing details with elements from other events and fictionalizing the rest.

Yet Streeter never told outright lies. Each of his anecdotes of bravery had a seed of truth. Rather than disregarding his colorful embellishments, this book offers them as "legends" for comparison with the facts. All quotations are given verbatim from their various sources, where they were subject to the chronicler's memory as well as falsification either to dignify what was said or to provide folksy entertainment.

Although the transformation of the north shore was largely secret and covered with an overlay of deceit, it is impossible to think of Chicago without it. Even when stripped down to what can be proven, the story of how this happened remains incredible.

PART I
A FORTUNE
AT STAKE

CHAPTER I
THE FIRMAMENT

Incongruously rising from the swamp, Potter Palmer's castle must have looked like an illusion until the new carriageway reached his door at 100 Lake Shore Drive, an address later changed to 1350 North Lake Shore Drive to conform with the rest of the city. Passersby must have dismissed the anomaly as just one more eccentricity of the rich.

Now the Lincoln Park Board needed to go through the motions of approving an extension across partly submerged lots that had just been secured by the investors' syndicate, something the state was years from authorizing. Contractor Charles Fitz-Simons's business partner, Charles Connell, seems not to have been involved in any part of the Lake Shore Drive plan, and in the early stages, the former general worked with a Scottish associate, Malcolm McNeill. Their immediate concern was winning over the last holdout, Tobias Allmendinger, and they stalked him like a vulture.

Having evidently originated part of the plan, the old German entertained an idea of how valuable his deed might become, but he did not want to die in debt. Allmendinger gave in on January 6, 1886, and handed over "for $5 and other valuable consideration" (a nearby lot not specified) one section of empty marshland near Oak Street and, for $40,000, eighty-six feet of shoreline and all riparian rights to build a pier or use for landfill.[1]

Although the Drive so far reached only a few blocks, from the park to Bellevue Place, the work was starting to arouse curiosity. It is in this tense atmosphere that an ill wind blew Streeter to the wilderness to start what

N.K. Fairbank's English granddaughter would call "a funny old legend for Chicago." First, here is Streeter's version, which until now has been accepted as fact.

Legend: The Shipwreck

Streeter and his wife, Maria, were running a steam excursion boat out of the working-class suburb of South Chicago. Unlike trains, excursion boats kept families together and usually had a piano player or band during trips to and from shoreline recreation spots in other Great Lakes states.

On Saturday, July 10, 1886, the couple took a private party of three people along with unknown cargo to Milwaukee, but an approaching gale forced the passengers to cancel their return trip. Streeter had been toying with the idea of sailing his top-heavy second-hand boat to Honduras to smuggle guns for insurgents. Why not plow through the storm to see if this brave little craft could take it?

The battle-scarred Civil War veteran hired a sailor from the Milwaukee docks, but "the damned fool was skeered to death." Maria became sick as they neared the Chicago shore. Knowing the city's concave lakefront "like the back of [his] hand," Streeter maneuvered the *Reutan* to a sandbar. He and Maria were thrown to the deck, and the engine broke. "We were then at the mercy of the wind and the waves, hopelessly drifting about."

Gusts drove the boat behind the breakwater after nearly crashing it against Farwell's little pier near Chicago Avenue. Waves broke over the deck as the anchor dragged across the sandy lakebed. Streeter tied a rope around his waist but in a five-hour ordeal was twice swept overboard.

At about three o'clock Sunday morning, the *Reutan*, heavy with water and sand, sank to the shallow bottom about 450 feet out. Every dollar the Streeters had was tied up in the vessel, and now even their lifeboat and life raft were swept away.

Shortly after dawn, two men on the beach noticed the empty lifeboat and came out to bring the skinny mariner and his wife ashore. That was when Streeter decided to build an island around the ruins of his vessel so that he and Maria would have a place to stay.[2]

So far, the story is plausible but contains little truth. Was there a gale? National Weather Service records show that the strongest wind in Chicago that day was twenty-three miles an hour, not uncommon in a midsummer storm. Was Streeter a battle-scarred veteran? Army documents disclose that as a member of the occupying force he saw just a few skirmishes. Streeter also claimed to have been wounded twice fighting the Rebels, but a letter he crudely wrote to the army for compensation gives his only injury as a back sore from carrying a heavy pack. Perhaps his sergeant had put rocks in the sack, a common punishment for lazy or belligerent soldiers. Streeter appears to have been both.

Chafing at orders, Streeter deserted soon after the Confederates surrendered and took his rifle with him. Army records have him being five foot six. But since he was usually seen in a top hat and oversized coat, even acquaintances could not agree on whether he was short or tall. Add to this his piping voice and oversized ambitions, and he seemed imagined by Charles Dickens or Bret Harte. Skinny as he was, events would show that he remained strong into his seventies.

Streeter was approximately forty-two when he settled on the shore and a failure at whatever he had tried. But he talked big. Because he had picked up a few legal terms, he called himself a lawyer; because he had patched up two excursion boats, he claimed to be a shipbuilder; and although he boasted about being a master seaman, there is no evidence he could swim. No doubt he would have loved to learn that generations of local historians actually believed him.

Even the name of his boat may have been fictional, as he called all of the others after women. In newspaper interviews and in the reminiscences of his friends, he never expressed any interest in foreign events. But since he had made up the gale, the Cap'n needed a reason for going through it. Typical of him, he misspelled the Honduran capital of Roatan.

The craft might not even have been an excursion boat. Since Streeter's base was the steelworker town of South Chicago, there was little demand for family trips to distant locations. There might, however, have been a need for a bumboat, providing liquor on the Sabbath despite blue laws, and some of these boats had cubicles for prostitution. We know that he tried to set up a bumboat years later. That Streeter would risk sailing to Milwaukee with a storm coming for just three passengers was also unlikely, unless the "private party" was quite some party.

The main question is not the nature of the boat but precisely where it foundered. The answer is that no one could have known even a few weeks later. Freshwater waves hit harder than ocean breakers, and they seldom strike that part of the city head-on. Before man-made beaches and individually designed breakwaters, storms would scoop away gobs of shoreline and leave behind narrow shoals lasting only until the next deluge.

The lake also was the farthest inland since settlers built cabins near Fort Dearborn at the river mouth, and no one had recorded the point where sand rose above the water since 1821. The closest charted sandbar was just off a cluster of factories immediately north of the river. If the rickety boat had bumped into that, Streeter could never have claimed the shore between Cedar Street and what is now Grand Avenue.

But how could someone who had never lived in the city and who scraped for money all his life know about a clandestine real estate

The stranded *Reutan*. How it became involved in the Lake Shore Drive development became a million-dollar mystery. *Captain Streeter Pioneer.*

arrangement? He might have seen Palmer's castle and distant seawall and possibly dredging or road construction equipment. We may infer from testimony in Streeter's 1902 murder trial over a gun battle on the land that hotheaded Fitz-Simons gave some of the secret away. This is what he told the jurors:

> *I was working as a contractor on shore when I noticed a little sloop being poled to the shore by a red-whiskered man. I saw he intended to tie up at the Farwell pier. I went out to the pier and, as he came alongside, I notified him not to make fast there, as it was a private landing and I was in charge of it. He paid no attention to me.*

Streeter, acting as his own lawyer even though his life was at stake, abruptly changed the line of questioning, virtually confirming Fitz-Simons's account. Both men must have been glad to leave the uncomfortable subject behind. So let's look at this testimony a little more closely.

The Cap'n would always say his boat had foundered hundreds of feet out, but Fitz-Simons testified that the defendant was able to pole it toward land, and the normally talkative Streeter declined to contradict him.

Why would the former general say he was in charge of that small private pier? And why was he "working as a contractor" on a Sunday morning in rigidly churchgoing times? More than likely, Fitz-Simons was protecting his own investment, and that would place him not near the Farwell or Fairbank property but closer to Oak Street, which the contractor had been eyeing as his own.[3] This would especially make sense because Oak Street was close to the office of Fitz-Simons & Connell.

Now we turn to the two men who, in Streeter's version, supposedly aided the waterlogged Streeter and his wife on the morning after their shipwreck—a Newberry watchman named Dugan and young De Witt Cregier Jr. Dugan appears to have been alone when he saw the couple poling their boat. Rather than offering help, as Streeter would claim, he evidently went to Fitz-Simons and asked what should be done about them. The contractor squished through rain pools and told Streeter not to tie his damaged boat to Farwell's landing. "Why not?" Streeter no doubt asked.

A few weeks before Streeter's arrival, Fitz-Simons had tried to shake off a reporter curious about the new construction by taking credit for an unspecified landfill plan, no doubt covering for Palmer on the spur of the moment. The contractor also told the reporter that Allmendinger was acting as his agent. Very likely this was the sort of thing Fitz-Simons blurted out to the stranded couple.

Whatever Fitz-Simons let slip, Streeter's underrated canniness took over. It would have been just like him to say something to put the marine engineer at ease and then do the opposite. Sometime after the general left, Cregier Jr. showed up. His father, who lived nearby, was the city engineer and would become an undistinguished mayor.

Since Streeter had been turned away from Farwell's land, he asked Cregier's help in bringing the boat onto shore some yards away. That was how the hull of the *Reutan*, or possibly the *Maria*, broke open on the sodden marsh secretly owned by Fairbank, who had founded or sat on the boards of the Chicago Symphony Orchestra, the Chicago Public Library and the annual music festival. Luckily for Streeter, of all the phantom shore owners, Fairbank was the one said to be "kind-hearted."

With considerable audacity, Streeter decided to maintain an unsightly presence and see what the millionaires might offer for him to go away. In the meantime, he would establish a claim by making the irregular shoreline even less clear. When Fairbank's lawyers arrived that Tuesday or Wednesday, they found that the squatter couple had moved into a shack, possibly one abandoned by Gregory Fritsche after forty years of tax-free living.[4] Streeter told them he and "Mariar" would need a day or two more to patch up their boat and they would be off.

Streeter would claim that he then acquired a yawl for ferrying garbage and dirt, presumably dug up for foundations and dumped on this splat of landfill off the above-water portion of Fairbank's property. In his self-spun legend, the Cap'n, with the help of cheap roustabouts, repeatedly traveled four hundred feet out and piled discarded bricks, granite street-paving blocks, chunks of sandstone and old railroad ties around the wreckage, raising the split hull a fraction per day.

Unlike the millionaires, he could not afford steam-driven sand-sucking machines to build his land. So he paid refuse drivers fifty cents a load to deposit garbage and construction debris off Superior Street, near where the towering John Hancock Center now stands. Contractor Hank Bresser would say at Streeter's murder trial that after outlining his scheme the Cap'n told him, "They'll have to buy us off. We'll get a million out of it!"[5]

There was no yawl, which would have meant a sail. Attorney Francis X. Busch, who would simultaneously be a casual friend and a professional enemy of Streeter's, recalled that Streeter just nailed together something like a barge propelled with push poles.

Streeter was perfectly suited for making a nuisance of himself, with his tobacco-stained beard, his fondness for profanity, his liquor-loving wife and his no-plumbing lifestyle. Yet inelegant as he was, the Cap'n was never crude and seems to have been only a moderate drinker. Whenever he ventured off the wasteland, he wore an old plug hat and a cutaway coat to ape dignity even if it made him look like a ringmaster.

By mid-autumn, the prosperous men behind the Lake Shore Drive plan must have had a chilling thought. What if the Streeters never went away? Rather than employing a show of force, as Palmer or Farwell might have done, Fairbank decided to speak to them without the intrusion of lawyers or constables.

Now in his fifties, Fairbank had a fringe of white hair that merged with his mutton chop sideburns. He had put on weight from his handsome and athletic youth but carried it well and remained commanding in appearance. Their confrontation shows that the dividing line between legend and fact sometimes depends on where you end the story.

Legend: The Fairbank Encounter

As Fairbank's buggy pulled off a dirt road, Streeter stepped down from the *Reutan* with an old army rifle.

"I want you off my land, that's what I want," Fairbank said as he stepped away from his carriage, looming nearly half a foot above Streeter, "and I'm giving you exactly twenty-four hours to get out!"

"Twenty-four hours," Streeter snorted. "Well, I'm going to give you just one minute to get the hell outten here before I shoot a hole through you. This is my land, and I'm going to stay here till hell freezes over. Now you get."

Fairbank threatened to torch the crippled boat, but Streeter warned: "I'll shoot your [side] whiskers off if you do. You can't work no Johnny Bull on me because I was born in Michigan an' your riparian rights is nothing to me."

Maria appeared and put in: "Our rights is more riper than his; more by token that we were here first."

At this, Fairbank hurried back to his buggy while cautioning, "I'll have the law on you, you old devil. You'll see."

"To hell with the law," Streeter answered. "There ain't no law that kin touch me. This is my land, and I'll kill any son of a bitch what says it isn't!"

—Adapted from Francis X. Busch, *Casebook of the Curious and True*, and a *Chicago Tribune* interview with Streeter, September 10, 1890

This certainly sounds like Streeter but nothing like Fairbank, who once led the lake rescue of one hundred people during a storm. A letter tucked away in Chicago Dock and Canal Trust files provides a believable longer version from Fairbank's friend Frederick M. Bowes. When Fairbank stopped his buggy at the boat ruins, Streeter indeed held a long-barreled weapon (Bowes said a shotgun, not a rifle) just inches from the tycoon and threatened to pull the trigger. But then Fairbank said, "Go ahead and shoot."

In the face of such courage, Streeter remarked, "Well, if that's the kind of man you are perhaps we can talk things over."

This evidently led Fairbank to believe that Streeter lacked the resolve to persist as a threat. As he would write to a newspaper, "I don't regard the efforts of Streeter as anything but a bit of comedy." But for the next few weeks, either Fairbank or middle-class shore owners from the Pine Street Association used legal badgering in hopes of discouraging the couple from staying.

One code enforcement officer after another informed them that they were violating an ordinance. The Cap'n might have paid a fine or two—any such records are long gone—but he stayed on. As he phrased it: "They ordered me off. I wouldn't go. They asked the Health Department to fire me, an' I fired the Health Department. They sent the Harbormaster to put me off, an' that didn't work."

He vowed to take the case through federal court to keep the city from evicting him. "And," he added, "if Uncle Sam don't fight 'em off, this ain't no land of freedom."

After perhaps three weeks of this, the city stopped sending people to hector the squatters. Since Streeter was no more compliant now than when he had arrived, the owners must have been afraid of pushing him too far. He might start shooting or, worse, file a suit. It seemed best to leave him alone.

Since Streeter's scheme for obstructing the Drive was working well, he tried a variation downtown. Learning that a skyscraper was about to be built at Adams Street and what is now South Michigan Avenue, he hired men to push an abandoned streetcar onto the property. Then he opened it as a diner, just to create an irritation. When the owner failed to protest, the Cap'n built a shelter over it. Rather than going through the trouble and cost of eviction, the owner bought off the scruffy intruder with several hundred dollars.[6]

The bankroll let Streeter think about hiring lawyers and paying more haulers to fill in his part of the shoreline. For the time being, he was claiming the "found land" (property built up from the lakebed) by right of Maria's being a Civil War widow. In reality, she didn't know whether she was a widow.

Since it would not take long for his enemies to discover that she never held government scrip entitling her to undeveloped land, Streeter invented a land warrant so that he could claim it had been "lost." Many years later, when an attorney at a civil hearing trial asked how he obtained the supposed warrant, Streeter answered in his squeaky rasp, "Why, my friend, I bought it from a man who owned a hotel down at Kentucky Lake, Indiana. I don't recall his name."

With his usual sense of humor, he also worked out an explanation for claiming his little island. The submerged land had not been on any map, making it undiscovered. When he built upon it and the land appeared above the surface, he saw it first, making it his by right of discovery. And since under international treaty the Great Lakes belonged neither to the United States nor Canada, out of patriotism he annexed the property to the United States.

Probably convinced that the shadow owners would never buy him off unless he did something outrageous, he began selling shares of his land (actually Fairbank's). The Chicago Real Estate Board repeatedly advised small-time investors that Streeter's claim was fraudulent, but nothing was done to charge him.

The millionaires had other concerns than a pair of squatters. In 1887, the Lincoln Park Board approved building the southern and much longer portion of Lake Shore Drive, bringing the carriageway and seawall from Bellevue Place all the way to Indiana Street (the straight portion of what is now Grand Avenue). This would take the road as far as it could go at the time because of a group of small factories near the river mouth. All that was needed now was state authorization.

Years later, attorney Henry I. Shelton would claim under oath that he was the original promoter of the Drive extension and that for two years he took "subscriptions" (investment money) from the Ogden estate, the Newberry family, Farwell and Fairbank. But, as with Fitz-Simons, he was fronting for the investors' syndicate.

To understand what was going on, we might look into disclosures arising from litigation in 1894. The Illinois attorney general charged that the North Shore Land Association—another Palmer front—"capitalized" a portion of the land yet to be made with $3 million.

Left unsaid was that the secret owners were expecting to reap vastly more than this. The carriageway district after all was never intended for "old money" families but for "new money" and the second generation of business leaders, with the landowners reaping fabulous rents from multiple-dwelling buildings that so far were only a gleam in Palmer's eye.

The state attorney general tried to have Shelton admit that at least two illegal acts were involved. One was that landfill for the second phase was laid two years before the roadway contracts were signed, which Shelton denied despite the facts. The other allegation was that Fitz-Simons had spoken at some of the park meetings. This would have been a double conflict of interest since he was in charge of construction and also had been surreptitiously promised made land off Ohio Street. Shelton avoided outright perjury by continually answering, "I have no recollection of that." As will be shown later, short memory was a constant in the project.[7]

But that state inquiry was years away. For now, in the autumn of 1886, no outsider had a clear idea of what was going on. Although at least three people had seen Streeter's leaking *Reutan* near the Farwell pier in July, it was somewhere farther out now. He may have wanted to simulate the ramming of a sandbar so that he could avoid assertions that he actually had landed on private property. If there had been no sandbar that summer, with all of Streeter's hasty refuse dumping, there was one in November.

All his efforts were illegal from the first time he splashed something into the water because Illinois statute required state permission before anyone could obtain title to landfill. The shore owners knew this, the city attorney knew this and the police knew this, but no one did anything.

Previously, a small, flat-bottomed boat could pass between Streeter's island and the mainland. Then he built a causeway of dirt and broken stones connecting them, further trapping sand and silt that otherwise would have been swept to the Indiana dunes.

Also in this period the lake began receding on its own. Soon no one could say how much land he actually had created, with the usual estimate being less than two acres. As the legend goes, so much property was accumulating around the boat that the envious "dollar hogs" were starting to claim the sand-land for their own.

Continuing to live in a fisherman's shack might have made Streeter and Maria trespassers in the eyes of the law. With winds turning brutal, the couple decided to make the wreckage their permanent abode. Sometime around Thanksgiving 1886, the Cap'n and probably some men hired from Clark Street dives for fifty cents a day put pine boards and jackscrews under the *Reutan*—or the *Maria*—and shoveled dirt and sand under the hull so that the remains were entirely out of the lake. Streeter did what he could to make it rainproof with planks and canvas, and Maria "fixed it up purty" with second-hand furniture.

No doubt there were also pots, a skillet, knives, spoons and perhaps pictures cut from newspapers, since this was how transients equipped their huts on the marsh. The Streeters may have heated their food on an open fire and taken occasional baths in the lake. We know they hung their wash on a clothesline stretched between two sticks in the ground. The couple had no privacy facilities other than the weeds. Remarkably, an entire year passed without incident.

If the Streeters ever had second thoughts about their extortion scheme, those ended in early 1888 when a ghost ship ran aground somewhere

Streeter in the workshop inside his scow fortress. *Captain Streeter Pioneer.*

close by. Great Lakes ship owners often let their insurance lapse as the wooden vessels aged and abandoned them after a final voyage in heavy weather. Other people would come along, look them over and convert salvageable ones into river barges towed down the Des Plaines and Mississippi Rivers.[8] The rest were left to the mercy of winds, currents and, in this case, destiny.

Streeter had the thirty-foot scow hauled to his irregular plop of landfill. Since Palmer had his castle a few blocks to the north, Streeter decided to turn this hulk into a fortress. One entered it by going up a ladder for a few feet and passing through a hole in the stern facing Fairbank's vacant landfill rather than the lake. After tearing away at the prow to fashion the rest into a porch, the Cap'n sawed through a few boards for windows.

The resulting structure looked nothing like a boat and something like a bilevel shanty. Some people mistook it for a barn, but he stocked it with enough weapons to do battle with the city.

CHAPTER 2

"A STRENUOUS CUSTOMER"

S treeter is a strenuous customer," Fitz-Simons would say of him a few years later. "He'd die within a week if he didn't have wildcats and rattlesnakes served up to him three times a day." The contractor, something of a showoff-ish rogue himself, added, "Really, nobody pays attention to him, and he seems to be fulfilling his aim to stir up fun for the public. Great card, is Streeter."[1]

Although the game would turn deadly, the Cap'n appears not to have been very serious in the early years. He enjoyed thumbing his nose at respectable people and living in a fantasy of outsmarting them.

His father, William, was a twenty-nine-year-old farmer when he married fourteen-year-old Catherine Marion in upstate New York. Like many of their neighbors, they came to believe that the Genesee Valley had become too crowded with the opening of a local canal. So they journeyed by boat and wagon to the seemingly endless forests of Michigan, where a settlement of fellow upstate New Yorkers named the county after their beloved river.

Although the Cap'n once stated that he was born in 1837, and so it is given on his simple grave marker, various records list it as being between 1841 and 1846.[2] Judging from photographs and Streeter's vigor in later years, this book assumes the birth year was 1842. Whatever it was, June 11 was his birthday.

Palmer, Fairbank and Farwell also came from upstate New York, but they were reared in the Congregationalist tradition of strengthening character for social development. The Streeters stressed pioneer self-reliance over self-mastery. Just clearing space for a home took a community effort with oxen, axes, handspikes, mauls, chains, ropes and pulleys.

Streeter's mother must have been a remarkable woman, bearing eleven children and living into her mid-nineties. But his maternal grandmother appears to have been the relative most fond of him. All his brothers and sisters lived out their lives on farms in the Genesee County area near Flint. The only other one known to have extended himself was Henry, who became a millwright as well as a farmer.

As a stick figure of a boy, George Streeter enjoyed playing with Indian children more than he did with his brothers and sisters. One imagines that they were too busy with farm work and household chores. He attended school only when not needed at home. Busch, author of *Casebook of the Curious and True*, believed that he had only a year, all told. Each February he and his brothers would pound spigots into maple trees and collect the dripping sap in wooden troughs to make syrup for the rest of the year. The boys spent those nights in lean-tos made from fallen branches. George enjoyed himself so much that he would prefer living outdoors the rest of his life.

For a while, Streeter's father augmented his farming income by serving as a justice of the peace, which required only a law book that no doubt George thumbed through with more fascination than comprehension. Disdaining farm work, the teenager patched barges and learned how to outfit them with a boiler and a deck.

Not wanting to be tied down, the lanky teen hopped aboard a neighbor's covered wagon, hoping for excitement. But he looked over the abandoned claims along the South Platte and headed back. Too bad, because a few who stuck it out became rich from silver veins running through the Colorado rocks.

Streeter was still living with the family when he was drafted into the Union army in November 1864, a few months before the war ended. His fictionalized autobiography has him taking part in the Battles of Lookout Mountain, Missionary Ridge, Knoxville, Chattanooga, Kingston, Goldsboro and Atlanta, all with hair's breadth adventures that he neglected to mention when seeking veteran's compensation for his fistula. Only two incidents in his book are convincing: ducking behind tombstones to escape enemy potshots and almost killing a farmer for a bag of beans.

Following Lee's surrender, Streeter was sent to a "tent hospital" in Washington, D.C. When his back sore healed, he was assigned to help keep the peace in Louisville. Ten weeks after Appomattox, he couldn't stand orders any longer. So on June 23, Private G.W. Streeter picked up his rifle and headed home. He never paid back the army for his rifle and "accoutrements."[3]

His peacetime desertion and reluctance to help out on the farm may have increased family tensions, and he longed to get away on his own. But dreamers make the worst businessmen. Envying the success of P.T. Barnum, Streeter traveled to Indiana with a menagerie of three deer, two moose, a buffalo calf and a pig he said weighed fifteen hundred pounds. "I billed this hog in my advertising literature as a white elephant, and I never heard anyone complain about being disappointed in this little fake."

When that failed, Streeter ran a circus by hiring a ventriloquist, a magician and a human pincushion and by adding a "drama troupe" that presumably comprised members of the acts and perhaps himself. He used the profits to buy lots around Flint, not that anyone wanted him back.

Streeter in his showman days before landing in Chicago. *Captain Streeter Pioneer.*

After the circus wagons became mired in the rainy spring of 1867, he sold all his Michigan holdings to pay off debts. Perhaps people living around the family farm were laughing at him. Everything he did afterward seems to have been a way of trying to prove that he could be a success on his own terms.

In time Streeter acquired a small steamboat already named the *Wolverine* and gave himself the title of captain, but pronounced it "cap'n." He would be called "Captain," "Cap" or "Cap'n" from then on. When the boat struck a rock in the Ohio River, everyone abandoned ship. Possibly not knowing how to swim, Streeter became separated from the others.

Drenched and trying to find shelter, he was surprised by a bear and stayed up a tree "for fully two hours." He was so hungry when he climbed down that he tried clubbing a fish in a muddy pool but fell down in the slime. He just couldn't do anything right.[4]

In the winter of 1875–76, he returned to the Flint area. He may not have found forgiveness, but he did find a flirtatious seventeen-year-old Canadian American girl named Lavina Walters. He called her Minnie, the first of four women in his life to have a name or nickname beginning with M: Minnie, Maria, Mary and Ma (Elma).

Late in life Streeter told a judge how this marriage came about (one can almost hear the laughter in court): "Minnie and me were out on a sleigh ride one night and there was company at all our relatives'. I just dropped the reins an' let the mare go. She took us to a house where there was a bunch of preachers, and Minnie said, 'Let's get married.' We did."

The approximately thirty-three-year-old Streeter gave his occupation as "attorney" and rechristened the *Wolverine* the *Minnie A. Streeter*. But soon it became clear that the bridegroom was no lawyer or shipbuilder. The young wife "decamped suddenly without notice, carrying with her [Streeter's] hard-earned cash and accepted an engagement on a vaudeville circuit."[5]

The Cap'n and one of his sisters took over a hotel and livery stable in Bedford, Iowa. To hear Streeter tell it, he often met Jesse James and had two brawls with bruisers sent by his competitors "for the purpose of retiring me from my business." Judging from later events in Chicago, we might suppose that he had bought stock on credit, and the fights were with deputies taking them back.

After selling the hotel, the Cap'n operated a vaudeville theater in Chicago for six months and then ran the Apollo Theater near city hall. Finally, with money in his pocket, he went in search for get-rich-quick schemes. In Detroit, he met and married Maria Mulholland.

As if through with unreliable women, Streeter had wanted a helpmate who would stay with him; her looks and degree of intelligence did not matter. So this thin Methodist ne'er-do-well of English stock proposed to a hefty Irish Catholic woman who always dressed as if attending a Sunday social. Yet somehow they seemed right for each other.

Maria was born in Michigan perhaps a year after Streeter. At fifteen she married a man who gave her two children and disappeared from record after joining the Union army. "She was fightin' Irish, skeered o' nothin'," the Cap'n would say. She also was "strong as an ox, a dead shot, and the damnedest best female companion a man ever had."[6]

One day he found a small rotting vessel and could picture it as a "showboat." This was to be the *Reutan*, or possibly the *Maria*. But if the Cap'n had been a better shipbuilder, there would have been no Streeterville saga.

Working off and on, he replanked much of the hull and installed a secondhand boiler and engine. The next time we hear of the Streeters, they were struggling through a storm in July 1886 on their way into Chicago history.

But this was a bad time for the emergence of a folk hero. From where they landed they could see lights of Cook County Jail just north of downtown and a little inland. Five prisoners were awaiting the hangman for inspiring the Haymarket Square riot in which eight policemen died from a bomb explosion and pistol shots fired in the confusion.

Chicago giants such as Potter Palmer, Marshall Field and *Chicago Daily Tribune* publisher Joseph Medill had hardened after the violence of the 1877 railroad strike, and the Haymarket mêlée made them even more reactionary. Liberal Presbyterian minister David Swing, whose followers included Fairbank, even declared that an "ironhanded monarchy" would be preferable to freedom that permitted disorder.

The condemned men had claimed to be anarchists but were merely fighting for improved working conditions across the country. One of them killed himself in his cell, and the others were hanged before a packed crowd of spectators the next day, November 11, 1887. The relatively short northern section of the carriageway lay only a few minutes away.

Since no one was living on the former marsh except Palmer and the Streeters, only the portions needed for constructing unpaved cross streets were being filled in.[7] But for the first time, north lakefront property that had been there one year would stay there the next. An entirely new kind of residential district was now possible.

With the shore growing, Palmer started to invite a few families to sublease his lots for stone mansions, beginning with Franklin McVeigh, a businessman and lawyer from New York City who was respected as "a scholar in politics." He belonged to the prestigious Chicago Club and would serve as President Taft's secretary of the treasury.

Allowing him to build an impressive home beside Lake Shore Drive was a way of telling everyone that this was the quality of person who would live in the new district. McVeigh gratefully tried to start a movement to rename the Drive "Palmer Boulevard," but Palmer squelched it.[8] Besides being an intensely private man, the hotelier never wanted his name publicly connected with the project, to avoid the equivalent of claim jumping or adverse public reaction to his all-encompassing plan.

The second person Palmer chose to live along the Drive was President Lincoln's only surviving son, Robert Todd Lincoln. Robert had shown such promise in his first five years that his parents pushed him intellectually and neglected him emotionally. He developed an incisive intelligence that made him a member of such major businesses as the Continental Commercial Bank, the Pullman railroad car company and Commonwealth Edison.

Determined to be socially prominent on his own, Robert Todd Lincoln arranged for witnesses to testify that his neurotic mother, Mary, was insane. She was kept in an Illinois mental hospital until she could be "restored to her reason" and cease being an embarrassment to him.

Palmer may not have liked Robert Todd Lincoln—who was a Republican, unlike Palmer's Democratic friends—but he needed the rising man's standing to further the image of the Drive as the finest place to live west of Manhattan. Although happier in the social and political circles of Washington and the old-money mansions of Europe, R.T. Lincoln needed Chicago as a power base. He moved into a newly completed home at 60 Lake Shore Drive, near the park named for his father. Not far from there, electricians were running wires for street lighting at the southern end of the park to make the new homes safer at night. R.T. Lincoln soon became one of Bertha Palmer's closest friends and was appointed U.S. minister to Great Britain two years later.

Such were the people from whom the Streeters were trying to extort money with their free-and-easy lifestyle. As if demonstrating their intention to keep residing off Superior Street, they began sprucing up the former hulk. From second-hand stores and possibly dumps, they were amassing the most possessions they are ever known to have had, including a piano and a cooking stove vented by pipes going through the roof. This meant they at last could have warm water for tub baths. The Cap'n also picked up a small female dog for companionship.

When they needed to go outdoors in wind and rain, the Streeters slipped into yellow canvas jackets called sou'westers and long rubber boots they kept upstairs with their guns. Yet it would seem that nature was on their side, for the winters from 1888 through 1909 were unusually mild by Chicago standards.

In June 1889, the Illinois legislature formally granted to the park board the title to the submerged land off North Township and Lake View and approved extending the Drive from Bellevue Place to Indiana Street (Grand Avenue). Work began soon afterward, although the contracts would not be signed until 1892, possibly to keep names and details from prying eyes.[9] The owners on record merely paid $100 per front foot for the landfill and ceded their riparian (technically, littoral) rights to have the board build the carriageway across it.

"What is 'reparian' rights?" Streeter would say. "'Reparian' rights is the rights to repair your shore when it's wore off by the water."

Streeter's scow-fortress was allowed to remain, although the park board did not blink at using dynamite at two o'clock in the morning to demolish an unauthorized pier, and city officials were evicting other squatters, such as Olaf Larsen. The Chicago Dock and Canal Company started dumping its own landfill material just south of the carriageway route. Police blocked the work until the city attorney's office decided that only the Illinois legislature could stop it, but that was only an assumption.[10]

A man named Samuel Avery tried to build a shack near the Streeter fortress in the spring of 1889. Either he just wanted to live by the shore or thought he, too, might be bought off. No fool, Streeter let him nail the hut together before claiming territorial possession and blasting away with his shotgun. Judging from the wound, Avery was nicked in retreat.

The Cap'n was left in possession of Avery's "boathouse" and was acquitted of assault on the ground that he had fired in defense of his property. This did not mean there was a ruling establishing his right to the land.

Left alone, the Cap'n was less crude than he seemed. For all his faults, he cultivated a kind of chivalry that was out of place as the century was nearing its cynical end. He was never known to fire at an unarmed man except Avery, he always gave fair warning before shooting and when he expected trouble he made sure any women were away from harm, even the fighting Maria.

Since the Palmer group was ignoring the Cap'n, from time to time the Pine Street Association of middle-class owners of land nearby sent "plug-uglies" to serve warrants for one violation or another. Such men were barroom brawlers, former mining camp boxers and dockworkers waiting out a winter.

Instead of discouraging Streeter, the harassment and brawls forged his soul. "I was in the mood for that sort of work just then, and many a constable, detective, and sheriff felt the butt of that old musket [rifle] about his head and many of them passed into the dreamland stage by the same route," he said.

Guilt or innocence meant little in the police courts he often faced. Jury fees were paid by the person being tried, so a defendant needed only to be entertaining for an acquittal. Stranger yet, men needed for jury duty before a 1903 reform were often grabbed near saloons. Someone needing fifty cents for a few more drinks would step outside and try to look sober.[11]

Palmer's carriageway was starting to draw international attention. As visiting Scotsman William Archer would write after a few more mansions were built:

> *Driving along the Lake Shore to Lincoln Park in the flush of sunset, you wonder that the dwellers in this street of palaces should trouble their heads about Naples or Venice, when they have before their very windows the innumerable laughter, the ever-shifting opalescence, of their fascinating inland sea.*[12]

There was still the problem of creating an attractive parallel boulevard to enhance and complete the shoreline property—that is, for a stately back door to the lake-facing mansions and eventual apartment towers, something that would also ennoble the cross streets between them.

With a genius for turning byways into great streets, Palmer imagined a 116-foot-wide macadamized thoroughfare called Lincoln Park Boulevard (later called North Michigan Avenue). The avenue would be a northward extension of Pine Street, which at the time was just a mud flat supporting a mixture of middle-class homes, some factories and an aging brewery. Pine Street residents were forward looking enough to ban businesses such as saloons and laundries.[13] But the street went unpaved for years, and when a surface was laid, it was only cinder blocks and 66 feet wide.

In a process similar to the way the investors' syndicate had bought up shore land, agents persuaded all the owners of land fronting Pine Street between Oak Street and Chicago Avenue to give the park board fifty feet with the assurance that the truncated remainder would rise in value.

As with any major project, there was a holdout. And so attorney Henry Noble Cooper, vice-president of Fitz-Simons's dredging company, posed as an independent speculator in discussions with E.B. McCagg, regional head of the United States Sanitary Commission, an aid society that was a precursor of the Red Cross. Cooper finally agreed to buy the northwest corner of Oak and Pine for $90,000, a small fortune.[14] But he well knew what he was doing, because he was the organizer for several out-of-town investors in the Lake Shore Drive project.

One landowner who was wondering what was going on was Ireland-born bishop Patrick Feehan. The shoreline between the park and Burton Place had, until recently, been a Roman Catholic cemetery. With three mansions sprouting up on the filled-in marsh, the future archbishop thought of plowing all those empty graves back into real estate. But the park board apparently feared this would compete with Palmer's plan.[15] Not realizing what lay behind the board's refusal to let him run sewer lines across archdiocesan property, Feehan took back his riparian rights and held out until a state court ruled against him.

Before contracts could be signed for creating Lincoln Boulevard in January 1892, park commissioners held sixty-six meetings with shore

The Cardinal's Mansion off Astor Street at North Boulevard, where the Astor Street development was conceived. *Author's collection.*

owners or their representatives, reflecting what must have been hundreds of hours of bickering and compromises between the investors' agents and the landowners. No such meetings were ever held for the considerably more important Lake Shore Drive.

Since Bishop Feehan had not been let in on the plan, he began selling lots on his own between Burton Place and the park, helping to create the grand Astor Street District.[16] After superstitious crews ran at the sight of overlooked skeletons, socially prominent people such as Mrs. Joseph Bowen had trouble finding men to finish the work.

Palmer could not control Astor Street, although it was little more than a block inland from Lake Shore Drive and therefore within the general boundaries of what he had in mind for transforming the North Side. Instead of individually designed mansions such as the ones that were going up here and there along the Drive, Astor Street was seeing construction of three-story Queen Anne, Richardsonian Romanesque and Georgian Revival town houses facing one another. Most were abutting one another on just twenty-five-foot lots, half the size for Prairie Avenue mansions.

Beautiful but architecturally crowded Astor Street, just inland from Lake Shore Drive. *Author's collection.*

The new town houses may have drawn "ahhs" from onlookers, but they were the sort of homes Palmer wanted to keep off the Drive. In addition, narrow Astor Street was covered with common asphalt rather than a more durable mixture of asphalt and crushed stone.

A short distance away, a few people who had bought lots from Streeter built shacks to establish residence. Unfortunately, we know nothing about them.

Now that Streeter was no longer being hectored by shore owners, he wanted to see how far he could go. He came up with a map laying claim to a strip of uneven shore about two hundred feet wide between Superior and Ontario Streets. Then he apparently walked to some law offices and jotted down names so that he could assert that these attorneys supported his claim.

"Captain," county superintendent J.S. Sheahan told him, "some of your land is still under water and I cannot approve the plat."[17]

But in one of those inexplicable decisions that favored the squatter, the recorder's office accepted it, and the trusted Rascher Company in New York included the plat of "Streeter's Land" in its 1891 insurance map of

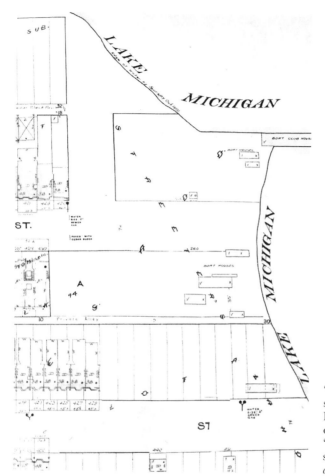

"Streeter's Land," as shown in the 1891 Rascher insurance map of Chicago, showing a "Club/Boathouse" and several shacks. *Author's collection.*

the city. This showed several transient shacks—even though most had been taken down—and listed Streeter's scow fortress as "Club/Boathouse."

While a judge considered Fairbank's suit against the Cap'n, absentee shore owners were so sure they were seeing the last of him that Farwell sent his son, J.V. Jr., to remove an ugly fence that the Cap'n had put up around his current estimate of what he had created, about four acres.

Streeter awoke that morning in October 1891 and saw policemen replacing the fence with lumber six to eight feet tall. The men were walling off the area he had specified in his plat rather than the amount he was now claiming. The Cap'n ran out and snatched one of the boards, but an officer knocked it from him and ordered the wagon driver to keep unloading.

Two policemen grabbed Streeter, patted him down and found a revolver in his pocket. As Streeter was being led away, smooth-faced Farwell Jr. told the workmen to pull down one of the remaining squatter shacks and evict a man who had been staying there, leaving the Streeters as the sole occupants of the disputed land. That made it easier to fabricate a heroic life for himself and his wife.

Evidently one night—we're not sure when—a drunk stumbled into the fortress to warm up until Maria threatened him, and he staggered out. Streeter wove this into a legend by turning the drunk into a villainous police officer.

Legend: Maria and the Chamber Pot

Maria was alone and screamed when she heard sounds in the dark. The policeman started up the ladder and yelled at her, "Come on down, you old [stew] pot."

She hopped out of bed, seized a chamber pot and flung its contents into the man's face. "If it's a pot you're looking for," she said, "here's one to remember me by!"

Streeter's supporters hurried in with shotguns and clubs, but by then the intruder had fled.

—Adapted from Francis X. Busch, *Casebook of the Curious and True*

Another day a constable and a few assistants caught the Cap'n in what he described as an "unguarded moment." Considering the sanitation facilities in Streeterville—none—we may imagine his composure when the leader ordered, "Come along, you." Maria emerged and poured a kettle of boiling water at him. In the confusion, the Cap'n snatched his rifle, and the would-be battle was over.

Wanting to improve upon reality, Streeter used this incident as the starting point for two tales, getting the axe from a later incident.

Legend: The Axe and the Boiling Water

(1) As Police Chief Joseph Kipley arrived with two dozen men, the Cap'n barricaded the scow door. "I didn't know they was police officers, and when they began battin' down the door I let fly with bird shot. They bruk down the door, though, and when one of them lunged in, Maria swung at him with an axe. It was a right hot fight for a minute or two—me pumpin' bird shot and swingin' my gun and Maria cuttin' at 'em with the axe—but they soon got enough and run out.

"Now, the papers said there was nine of the gang went to the hospital. One lost an eye, and two others had axe cuts." A jury picked from saloon row thought the Streeters were justified and acquitted them.

(2) Another time, "five rough-lookin' bastards with some kind of phony badges on" caught the Cap'n off guard and marched him out of the scow. "But they hadn't figured on Maria. She heerd the commotion and came to the top o' the stairs with an ole sawed-off shotgun, and filled their pants full of birdshot. They left in a mighty big way, but hollered to us they'd be back. I didn't believe 'em, but we took no chances and was ready for 'em. Sure 'nuff, they did come back. We gave 'em a hot reception. Maria and I was in the upstairs. Every boiler, pot and pan we had was filled with boilin' hot water, and when they got up to the house we emptied it on 'em as fast as we could. God how they hollered. They made off pronto, and that was all for that night."

—Both adapted from Francis X. Busch, *Casebook of the Curious and True*

Such shenanigans were still possible in a city retaining frontier elements, but the exciting days of individualism were ending. Mayor Hempstead Washburne made Chicago the first American city to adopt army-style drill for mass police deployment. More than efficiency was on his mind. Washburne wanted to prove that he knew how to crush threats to commerce.

In November 1891, a handful of policemen stormed a labor hall when a single member of the thousand workers inside insulted the flag.

Two days later, a squad of officers smashed down the door of another hall during a Haymarket Riot memorial and clubbed all who protested. Police Inspector Michael Schaak said labor agitators had become more dangerous because they "now have a certain class of sympathy they never had before." In one of Streeter's tales, he humbled the feared officer.

Legend: The Cap'n and the Inspector

"I looked out of my window on the old scow one night and saw Capt. Schaak and Officer Kehoe approaching my premises as they passed under a street light, and surmised they were up to some trick...so I slipped out, musket [shotgun] in hand, and hid behind a short stretch of fence about ten feet high...I sprang at them like a tiger and delivered a knockout blow on the head and shoulders of Schaak, who dropped like a log. Then I sprang on Kehoe, shouting at him as I did so, 'I've got you now!' But the latter ran as fast as he could in the direction from whence he had come, and then returned to attend the captain, who had recovered the use of himself, and was running as fast as his condition would permit.

"I let him go, but shouted dire threats and imprecations at him at the top of my voice."

—From E. Guy Ballard, *Captain Streeter Pioneer*

The Cap'n was ever talkative and congenial, and he kept his land (actually, Fairbank's) open to anyone dropping by. One of the livelier times must have been when about fifty American Indians encamped on their way to Michigan. Since this was bound to arouse suspicion that he was plying them with liquor to get them to sign over any shore rights they might have, Streeter told reporters tongue-in-cheek that his visitors were Siberians. Their visit may have been why he claimed in future years to have bought a deed from them.

The man being called the "Robinson Crusoe of the Lake-Front" whiled away his time puttering in a carpentry shop he had created on the ground floor of the scow fortress. He also patched up a few small boats so that he might run a ferry business when the 1893 world's fair opened on the south lakefront.

As he worked, loafed and even as he slept, the value of the shore kept rising. From $160 a front foot in 1882, around when Palmer started thinking about changing the nature of the North Side, the value jumped to $800 in 1892, even though the carriageway had not yet been brought across Streeterville.[18] Over the next seven hundred days, the land would be worth $1,500 a front foot.

Who would think that after six years of squatting Streeter would suddenly become an actual threat? A local court threw out Fairbank's trespassing suit, and the Illinois Supreme Court sustained the decision. One factor must have been that Fairbank's attorneys could not explain the true nature of Streeter's claim without divulging the park board's complicity in Palmer's scheme. A U.S. Supreme Court ruling in the Cap'n's favor would doom the entire project, and Streeter would be living beyond the dreams of avarice.

And so all those days of rain and snow, of heat and wind and subzero cold, of fog and blinding sunshine, those wistful smoky autumn hours— everything had at last paid off for the man who could never do anything right. Not only had the impossible happened, but it had also been upheld!

People started walking from downtown offices and strolling by from the Dearborn Street streetcar stop a few blocks away to talk with this whiskery man who had made shore out of firmament, this commoner challenging what he called the "Two Million Club"—such people as old Wilson, grandfather of future reporter Robert J. Casey. We can imagine Streeter's blue eyes dancing as he spoke about "valuable proppity," titles and foot values. The two men then shook hands, and Wilson led the boy back to the streetcar stop.

But like a lot of Chicagoans at the time, Grandfather Wilson must have considered the court decision a fluke and thought Streeter might not be able to maintain possession, if only because the millionaires had the police on their side. But for now, Streeter was doing what he did best: living as if on the frontier and concocting wild stories with his dime-novel imagination.

A Fortune at Stake

Legend: The Big Fight

The Swedish janitor at a downtown club overheard millionaires plotting Streeter's death. They would hire thugs, as the Cap'n told it, to "hand me my passport to the Great Beyond."

As they approached before dawn, "I promptly challenged their presence… and shortly thereafter advances on their part were met by defensive blows on my part. I made a great deal of noise, and this aroused the people who lived in the neighborhood to the westward [just off the lake].

"Finally, after many blows had been struck, they made a rush for me, and I retreated in good shape, climbing up the steps [ladder rungs] of my scow, on which my house was built. [The entrance] stood about three feet above the ground, hence the necessity for steps. I had my trusty musket handily placed for use at the top of these steps…I seized my old musket, which I had previously well loaded with an extraordinary amount of small shot, and gave them two charges at close range from different angles as they were trying to get aboard at the bottom of the steps.

"Never in my life have I seen so many pairs of shoes sticking up in the air at one time as on that occasion. It seemed to tumble every one of them to the earth…Doctors on the North Side were kept busy for several hours picking these small shot from different portions of their anatomy."

—Adapted from E. Guy Ballard, *Captain Streeter Pioneer*

CHAPTER 3

DISCLOSURES

With erosion being held in check by an Army Corps of Engineers breakwater and two short seawalls, Lake Shore Drive was crawling toward the Loop from Bellevue Place. Plans called for driving full-length pilings into the lake bottom at depths of six to twelve feet. Laborers under Fitz-Simons's direction sawed them off just below the water line, laid a platform of oak planks across them and eased concrete sections in an unbroken line.[1] After landscaping, the road was too impressive for just a carriageway; it was the city's newest boulevard.

Long before "gentrification" became a common term, middle-class residents from the Pine Street area were grumbling about the expensive new street going up for the rich. So they lent the Lincoln Park Board land for a temporary park that the *Chicago Daily Inter-Ocean* predicted would become the "garden spot of Cook County."[2] This was a time when Chicagoans cared so little for beautification that a woman named Sweet received a death threat when she campaigned for street cleaning.[3] The park shrank as more residences were built, and eventually it disappeared.

Apart from landscaping for mansions and landfill for cross streets, much of the route was still a blight of deep ditches. In time, all these trenches were filled in and graded. Although Palmer did all he could to keep us from knowing his role in all this, biographical sketches written privately for his family capture the scope in phrases at times paralleling Genesis:

The South shore was sure to be occupied by large manufacturing plants, but the North shore seemed destined to be covered with palaces and villas, parks and pleasure grounds for public and private use. A boulevard along the north shore would command access to all the beauties of art [architecture] *and nature combined. When this magnificent boulevard was first laid out* [in Lincoln Park] *in 1873, his unerring judgment foresaw that it had the most brilliant possibilities as the most beautiful avenue of the city.*

Without hesitation he made extensive purchase of vacant land bordering upon it. The whole territory was a vast waste, but Mr. Palmer had it filled in…brought in the black earth, planted trees, forced the improvement of streets, encouraged the Lincoln Park Commissioners to come outward….This required some one person who had large property interests, that the work might be well and properly done. [He] *gave of his wealth to the making of the famous Lake Shore drive, invited the best of people to form a community where there had been a wilderness and set his home in what is now the most beautiful section of the city…This took years, but the work was willingly done.*

Let it be written, "He builded for men."[4]

On a single day a reporter positioned at another part of the route counted twenty-seven wagons unloading everything that could be shoveled onto a mound, including cinders, kitchen refuse, butcher shop garbage and stable manure "warm and steaming." Unsuitable materials such as dead chickens were pulled out and fed into a bonfire, filling the air with smoke and stench.[5] The Cap'n was the worst offender, if only because he covered each new refuse strata off Superior Street with a thin layer of dirt to look as though he were complying with an ordinance against using animal carcasses.

Upon these heaps was built at least part of "the most beautiful avenue in the city" and still one of the most impressive streets in the country. To enhance the panorama, the stark lines of the metal seawalls were softened by a narrow shoulder of sand.

Although the boulevard was hardly more than the size of a postage stamp when placed on a two-and-a-half-foot map of the city, in time it would inspire Chicago's unbroken line of artificial beaches.

A Fortune at Stake

The Streeters must have watched with more than idle curiosity, as the Drive inevitably crawled across their land under the hands of hard-muscled men and the continual tread of wagons. The Cap'n whimsically filed a suit to stop any construction without his permission, but he admitted that the road considerably improved his "propitty."[6]

The Drive was moderately landscaped with grass and narrow trees, but then all roadwork ended abruptly in a pile of construction material. The explanation lies at the heart of how we know any secrets of Lake Shore Drive.

Soon after Governor John Peter Altgeld took office, he replaced questionable park commissioners who had improperly authorized the boulevard with men of integrity. One new appointee, Horatio May, happened to live on Astor Street. He noticed during an amble along the lake in June 1892 that the pilings were "way away out of line" at Oak Street, the section that we now know had been promised to Fitz-Simons.[7]

May reported the irregularity to park superintendent John A. Pettigrew, who did nothing. So the younger man brought it up with other new members, and they determined that crews had gone between 135 and 150 feet too far, creating an alarming bulge. In effect, this was a land grab on top of another. The legislature ordered all construction immediately halted pending an inquiry into every aspect of funding and building the boulevard.

All this interest pushed the Lincoln Park Board into publicly admitting the Drive's existence by providing details of the project for the first time in its annual report issued on January 1, 1893, eleven years after Palmer began developing the lakeshore.

Now that the road had been built across Fairbank's land at Superior Street, the public benefactor renewed his effort to evict the Streeters, despite the state supreme court ruling allowing them to remain. The Cap'n had backed down at their only face-to-face meeting, but the man who had then seemed a Michigan yokel was now a court-savvy fighter.

Authorities waited until the Cap'n had left the area. At 10:00 a.m. on February 8, 1893, Maria looked up from whatever she was doing and saw Constable Charles Vogle at the head of a small army of carpenters, wagon drivers and hired men. "You get out of here!" she called out.

"The Captain will be home pretty soon now and he will shoot every one of you rascals."

Vogel went through the makeshift fortress and started handing furniture to his assistants. Their orders were to leave the Streeters with only their basic personal possessions. The carpenters even demolished part of the second level so they could send the piano down a plank. The instrument clanged in discord as it thumped against a mass of possessions on the ground. Vogel rounded up the Cap'n's puppies and put them in a box.

Helpless to stop so many men, Maria ran downtown for her husband. The Cap'n came back and was aghast to see his home ripped open and wagons laden with what looked like enough boards to rebuild Fort Dearborn. Streeter's answer was to sit on an overturned tub that had been pitched to the ground and watch as workers carried out the iron cooking stove, still hot, and nailed together forty-foot sections of planking.

Amid piles of clothes and papers, he buried his whiskered face into his hands. But what seemed like despondency was cold hard thinking. The Cap'n looked up and scanned what was on the ground, judged distances and sought areas no one was watching. He edged up a mound of belongings and slid out two Winchesters and three navy revolvers. He walked unnoticed into his small workshop and shoved the guns under an old carpet. Then he nonchalantly stepped out of the scow with the carpet rolled under his arm.

Amid the hammering he boarded a small boat that was part of his patched-up fleet, *Mariah the Squatter*. While teamsters drove a wagon of his things along a track of boards, Fairbank's attorney Byron Boyden wondered why the Cap'n was being so quiet. And there was Maria joining him. Something was up.

The Cap'n poked his rifle through the window of the icebound boat, and both squatters spewed profanities. The workmen dropped their nails and ran across the frozen ground. Streeter danced in joy on the ice and fiercely shouted a curse that accounts of the day represented with "——!"

"Now, don't get excited," Constable Haskins said as he darted behind a corner of the fortress.

"By all that's living, you can't take me!" the Cap'n shouted. "Ye're the hired tools of rich men; slaves and dogs paid to ruin Cap Streeter, but you can't do it!"

Two dozen laborers cowed as the Winchester made a slow sweep, and two policemen refused to step closer. Boyden left in disgust and came back with a warrant for Streeter's arrest. Officer Kerr timidly approached with the paper, ordered the Cap'n to surrender and took no for an answer.

The policeman walked a few blocks back to the East Chicago Avenue station for reinforcements. He returned not with a body of troops but with Captain Barney Baer. The large officer assured Streeter that if he surrendered he would be released on bond in a few hours. After sending Maria to find their attorney, probably one of those undereducated lawyers who could be found in certain shabby upstairs offices downtown, the Cap'n quietly gave up his guns and was taken away.

With the Streeters gone, carpenters finished setting up the stockade on three sides of the now reduced claim, with the lake being the fourth. Horses dragged *Mariah the Squatter* onto Superior Street, and the boat was left there.

The Cap'n went home from the lockup and knocked down a guard who had been posted to keep him from touching his boats until they could be sold at auction. Next, he removed a concealed rifle from under the weatherboarding of his fortress and told Constable Haskins and his two assistants to clear out.

The approximately fifty-year-old squatter climbed atop one of his upside-down boats and fired through a window of the fortress. Haskins and his assistants threw themselves to the floor and surrendered "unconditionally." When they emerged, Streeter ordered them to take to ice fringing the lake. After the assistants scattered, the Cap'n flourished his gun and threw sticks and bottles at Haskins's back to keep him walking.

With the help of friends, Streeter tore down part of the stockade and put back everything he could. But where was Maria? Locked up for public drunkenness and beating a policeman.[8] But in Streeter's version, his beefy wife was menaced by scoundrels.

Legend: Cap'n to the Rescue

One evening while Streeter was buying supplies, a boy informed him that five deputy sheriffs had seized the ground floor of the fortress and Maria was trying to hold them off. Seeing them "laughing and joking about the easy manner in which they had out-generaled me," he fired a shot that shattered the lamp. In the darkness "I poured a devastating and deafening round of shot into their midst, and at the same time yelled like a Comanche." The men exhausted their ammunition and begged for mercy.

The Cap'n kicked in the door and ordered them to clear out one at a time. As each man jumped out the doorway, Streeter punched him on the neck or shoulder with the butt of his shotgun. "All dropped to the sand without a murmur or a sound."

Two of the men ran half a mile in the "cold anchor ice and sought refuge in the Chicago Avenue water works pumping plant." The three others lay unconscious. Streeter gave the driver of a horse-drawn cab three dollars to take them to a hospital.

—Adapted from E. Guy Ballard, *Captain Streeter Pioneer*

Once crews knocked down the fortress with sledgehammers, sections to be reused by the city were dropped off at the foot of Randolph Street, where Mayor Washburne had created a temporary municipal dump near where Millennium Park now stands.

The only thing of value Streeter had left was his phony plat. With this as collateral, he borrowed money and bought a vacant lot at Seventy-third Street and South Vincennes Avenue, as well as an eight-flat across the street, where he set up a grocery on the ground floor.[9] Never mind that Streeter would swear in court several times that he had lived on the disputed North Side land exclusively.

Like many exiles, he was plotting his return. He had help from an unlikely source: the courts. In March, Judge Ewing dismissed Fairbank's

Streeter and Maria sitting outside their tent home after one of their many evictions. *Chicago History Museum.*

eviction suit against the Streeters on the grounds that the claim had not been made by Fairbank but by his agent and that the Cap'n had been "disposed of property" not specified in the complaint.[10]

The investigative *Chicago Times* knew that Maria would be more open about how her husband was earning money than he would be. During what seemed like a casual conversation, she mentioned that in the summer of 1891 a lawyer, two real estate developers and several others had talked the Cap'n into a scheme that would make his claim of four acres worth thousands of dollars by shady transactions existing only on paper.

The newspaper reported that the conspirators formed the North American Deposit & Investment Company, which divided Streeterville into twenty-five lots. The members "bought" and "sold" these lots back and forth among themselves without money changing hands. This way they jacked up the price to $10,000 apiece.

After the story came out, the county recorder's office held that the company "could not show a shadow of title to the land," and the partnership fell apart, leaving Streeter not much better off than before.[11] And so deputy sheriffs arrived one cold evening to seize all his grocery stock.

The couple cordially invited Deputy C.J. Jones upstairs for a meal. Tired of waiting alone, he came down and found Streeter pointing a shotgun at his face. Maria opened the door, and Jones quickly disappeared into the winter.[12]

The following Monday, deputies broke in with a ram of two-by-fours. Two friends who arrived just as the Streeters were being hauled away tried to help them escape but were roughed up and thrown into a cell. Charges were soon dropped, and it was safe to return.

Since the city had taken away his patched-up boats, the Cap'n chartered the *Mary Q* excursion boat and sailed North Side visitors to the Columbian Exposition fairgrounds at Jackson Park, selling lager beer and entertaining them with nonstop chatter that ended in a sales pitch.

On May 3, 1893, just two days after the world's fair opened to a dazzled throng, state senator Henry Bartling began a subcommittee hearing downtown to probe the nature of Lake Shore Drive. The inquiry was sparked by Fitz-Simons's blatant greed, although the mystery of why Streeter had not been driven off may have whetted the panel's curiosity. Bartling contended that the project was "an illegal deal" involving a park road that "leads to nowhere."

The subcommittee had no enforcement power, and its potential impact was already blunted by the death just the week before of park chief Charles Goudy, Palmer's inside man. Goudy was known for pushing propertied interests through the courts and was himself wealthy from land speculation.

An early disclosure was that ex-board secretary E.S. Taylor's salary virtually doubled in the period when the Drive was under consideration, that his meeting notes suddenly became meager and that really important matters were barely mentioned at the public sessions.

Goudy's second in command, Joseph Stockton—whose integrity Governor Altgeld doubted—testified that he knew nothing about how the Drive came to be authorized.[13] More barefaced lying came on May

11, when Fitz-Simons was asked to enlighten the senators on how he had made a slip of the slide rule and had his men pound pilings into navigable waters.[14]

Fitz-Simons attributed the oversight to difficulty in determining an agreed-upon boundary from an irregular shoreline, a problem that never came up when plotting landfill property for all the others. Like Stockton, Fitz-Simons said he couldn't remember when the contracts were signed, whether he personally went to any park board meetings or even whether he had tried to influence the commissioners.

The senators also had to threaten legal action to learn the names of the phantom owners. Even so, they needed to wait a week and a half before the list was handed over, and then it was suspiciously incomplete. The list showed that:

- the shore from the end of Indiana Street (Grand Avenue) to Ohio Street belonged to the estates of millionaire reaper inventor Cyrus McCormick and businessman William B. Ogden, the city's first mayor. The land was a block wide and almost half a mile long.
- the shore from Ohio to Ontario Streets was owned by the Ogden estate alone. It was a block wide and almost half a mile long.
- the shore from Ontario to Erie Streets belonged to the Ogden estate and several people who were never disclosed, possibly including department store magnate Marshall Field. This was a block wide and 2,527 feet long.
- the shore between Erie and Huron Streets was the property of Jessica N. McCreery, Potter Palmer, attorney Horace A. Hulbert and the Newberry family. This segment was one block wide and 2,390 feet long.
- the shore from Huron to Superior Streets was owned by N.K. Fairbank and the Newberry family. It was a block wide and 2,053 feet long. There was no mention of Streeter's claim, although he was still living there and selling lots.
- the shore from Superior Street to Chicago Avenue belonged to John V. Farwell. It was a block wide and 2,118 feet long.
- the shore from Chicago Avenue to Pearson Street was listed as "made land" surrounding the Chicago Avenue pumping station and was pledged to the city.

- the three-block stretch between Pearson and Walton Streets had no owners listed, but later events showed that they included the family of the late portrait artist George Healy and—what a coincidence—Lincoln Park Board commissioner DeWitt Cregier Sr., a future mayor.
- the shore between Walton and Oak Streets also had no ownership yet. Among the half-dozen parties interested were the North Side Land Association, the Chicago Title & Trust Company and Charles Fitz-Simons.[15]

As soon as the panel members got their hands on the list, they lost interest for no recorded reason, and not one shore owner was called to testify. Perhaps someone privately explained to the senators that much of the rents would be put into a charitable trust.

The hearing continued without any testimony of extra-legal conduct. But Stockton not only lied outright by saying he had no advance knowledge of the project; he also claimed the eventual cost of the extension would be $500,000 and that the developed land would be worth no more than $6–8 million to the shore owners. Some outsiders—though unaware of how extensive Palmer's concept was—were already putting the value at $12 million.

The only real consequence of the hearing was that the park commissioners ordered Fitz-Simons to uproot the wayward pilings and place new ones as close to the agreed-upon line as possible or face state action. Because of the landfill already created, he still gained a seventy-two-foot extension of his promised section, surely one of the most lucrative rewards in the history of bad math.

You can easily see the result of his larceny today on an ordinary Chicago map by looking at how Oak Street Beach bulges away from the natural curve of shoreline. This broad arc in fact needed a street of its own to connect the two segments of North Lake Shore Drive. This is short East Lake Shore Drive, with its exclusive residences and the plush Drake Hotel.

One point raised at the hearing was that the investors originally wanted the entire Drive half a mile farther into the lake so that it might extend behind the small group of factories near the river mouth. Legislators favoring the authorization bill backed down only when warned that this would unlawfully impede Great Lakes shipping.

Attorney Henry I. Shelton, who had fronted for the phantom owners, testified in the final days of the investigation that the four-lane boulevard and thirty-foot-wide promenade would be worth $40 million as a city asset. "When we are under the daisies," he said, "future generations will enjoy the fruits of our labors in the making of the shore drive"—his one true statement.[16]

The legislators noted in a preliminary report that despite the stated intention of serving the public, the road was essentially a private driveway for the rich, and its message to the working class was, "Keep off the grass." Indeed, there were no provisions for the general public. The panel concluded that although the Drive was improper and the behavior of Fitz-Simons was questionable, the boulevard so enhanced the city that any opposition would be insane.

In writing up their findings, the senators charged no criminal conduct but denounced the inadequate board proceedings under Goudy. "Inadequate" in those days was a gentleman's way of suggesting illegal conduct. Since Goudy was dead, it was safe to blame everything on him. In addition, Superintendent Pettigrew was asked to resign for refusing to take action when notified that Fitz-Simons had disregarded his blueprints.

Illinois attorney general Maurice Moloney was so incensed by the weak results of the hearing that he set up a Loop headquarters primarily to conduct his own inquiry. One day, Fitz-Simons, plump and fuming, stormed in and pounded on a desk to denounce him for snooping into private matters. This led to a fight in which Moloney, according to Fitz-Simons, "jumped up and caught at me. I avoided him." The contractor stormed back out only after being threatened with arrest.

With his Irish brogue, Moloney announced on February 20, 1894, that he was filing a suit against the board and the newly revealed shore owners. He charged that the park commissioners had no right to grant the lakebed to anyone, even for public use and certainly not to enrich the already rich. He threatened to rip out the entire carriageway and return the shore to a wilderness.

The attorney general brought to court what a newspaper called "a barricade" of charts and maps to outline his accusations, but the interests of the investors' syndicate were now being represented by the formidable Chicago Title & Trust Company. A parade of witnesses beclouded the issue, and attorney Shelton falsely claimed he had originated the extension idea. He put the year at 1887, long after Palmer had set the plan in motion.

Each time Moloney brought up the fact that construction began four years before state authorization, shore-owner attorneys stood up with objections. A lawyer for the Ogden heirs said they had paid the board $200,000 to fill in their portion of the shore and that reports of what the land was worth were vastly overstated.

When Moloney showed Fitz-Simons his own records pertaining to pilings and stonework for the breakwater, the marine engineer claimed he had no recollection of them. When Moloney brought up contracts Fitz-Simons had signed, the Ogden lawyer called the documents irrelevant.

In the end, Judge Windes ruled against the state. Only when his decision was upheld by the Illinois Supreme Court were the deeds taken out of escrow and released to the shore owners. That freed Fitz-Simons to buy the "made land" that had been calling to him off Ohio Street.[17] Whatever amount he paid, no doubt it was a bargain, considering his invaluable services.

Over the next few weeks, Fairbank's daughter, Helen, repeatedly visited Chicago's world's fair on the South Side. Riding a gondola across the lagoon with her girlfriends, she was unaware of the personal crisis her father was undergoing. Fairbank's closest friend in the Prairie Avenue district, erudite lawyer Wirt Dexter, had just died, and the country was sliding into a financial panic. This crushed Fairbank's hopes of cornering the pork market, after he had spent thousands of dollars on his Gold Dust Twins soap company, a railroad and an Arizona mine.

In the closing days of the Columbian Exposition, on October 28, 1893, portly mayor Carter Harrison answered a knock on his front door and was shot to death by a demented young man who believed he should have been appointed chief city attorney. After holding the world's attention for five months, Chicago was on a downward slide.

PART 2
SOVEREIGN
OF THE SAND

CHAPTER 4
CONSPIRACY

R eal estate had become the passion of the prairie. As soon as 1894 began, a number of lower-middle-class men and women began talking to lawyers about the validity of Streeter's claim and were usually advised to obtain an abstract of title. That is, a digest of landownership as taken from public documents. One such hopeful approached attorney Francis X. Busch, who was sure that Streeter was a fraud but who befriended him anyway and has left us a bemused account of the scalawag.

> *Everything about him suggested strength, determination and assurance. His shoulders were broad and his arms—perhaps because they protruded so far out of his sleeves—seemed abnormally long. He was straight as a ramrod and walked with a firm step, head well up….He wore a mustache, unkempt and so saturated with tobacco juice that no opinion about its natural color could be based on the evidence. I knew his hair in the early years had been carrot red. It was streaked with gray now.*[1]

What struck Busch most was the squatter king's hat. "It never sat squarely on his head, but held on precariously, pushed back from his forehead rakishly angled to the right." Streeter would take it off in court only if the judge insisted upon it. When he did, the reason for the hat became apparent: he was growing bald.

Such was the character on whom hardworking clerks and schoolteachers were pinning their hopes. In one of his fibs about land sales, the Cap'n said, "I never take less than $10,000 a lot for them," but we know that some prospective buyers were trying to raise just $5,000. With his new prosperity, he bought a beaver hat and took to smoking cigars rather than chewing tobacco.[2]

The Cap'n told Busch that his deed from an Indian tribe (sometimes the document was described as a soldier's scrip) had been lost in the U.S. General Land Office. Busch was sure the colorful scamp was lying, and on a trip to Washington, D.C., he confirmed that no such document existed. Streeter was unaware that a notation was made of every document received.[3]

Streeter never sought out reporters, but when they showed up, he had a little fun with them. After J.D. Birdsell, a hotel owner in South Bend, Indiana, expressed an interest in purchasing a lot, the Cap'n told them the investor belonged to the famous Studebaker carriage family in that town. "We will surprise you next summer," he added. "We will have a city of our own up there—water, gas, electric lights and policemen…and the Two Million Club will be glad to annex us as soon as it needs us."[4]

As with big businesses, major real estate development was passing from strong-minded individuals to corporations, assuring a fight to the finish because a board of directors never gives up. But the middle-class owners of land just west of the Drive and between Pearson and Walton Streets were chafing under Streeter's continued presence. Acting on their own, they hired Henry N. Cooper to serve as both policeman and spy. Cooper, formerly a Palmer agent, enters the story as a shadowy figure, appearing, like Mephistopheles, only in times of crisis.

As counsel for the Pine Street Association, he worked with the North Town(ship) Board on property matters pertaining to the former marsh.[5] This kept the association abreast of each infraction, from lot selling to loud partying. Cooper's eight years of surveillance would climax in a fatal shooting.

Yet the Cap'n made no effort to stay out of trouble. Reporter Robert Casey recalled an eviction attempt in the summer of 1894. When half a dozen deputies crossed the landfill where Streeter had a shack, he "filled the legs of three of them with buckshot." This brought a squad of police a week later, and a sergeant talked him into surrendering on a charge of assault with a deadly weapon. "The judge accepted his plea that the buckshot wasn't deadly," Casey wrote, "and that the question of who owned the lake front wasn't the issue at point."[6]

By 1895, the *Chicago Times* was calling for a South Lake Shore Drive similar to the one on the North Side. But the talk in exclusive clubs and Loop barber chairs was less about land and investments than it was about money. That July, more than four hundred Chicago Democrats chartered a train and rode down to the state capital in Springfield for a raucous parade in favor of the silver standard. "These Chicago Democrats are 16 to 1," a correspondent wrote. "Sixteen parts whisky and one part water."

Until now, Streeter had operated with caution, but in this money-mad year he almost overreached himself. In early May, he went to Washington and tried to have the U.S. General Land Office accept a homestead entry of "150 acres more or less" (though he had earlier claimed 4 acres and was restricted by the city to 2). The application was rejected because the property was the same that had been turned down in March of the previous year, when he had claimed the area as a military-bounty land warrant.

Far from being unproductive, the visit led the Cap'n to fellow Chicagoan William Cox, and they would engage in fraud as if it were a vaudeville act. Credit for the meeting goes to a supposed physician and minor businessman named Jacob Nine, who seems to have enjoyed staying in the background so that he would have clean hands if things fell apart.

For some time, Cox had emulated Streeter but did not want to work as hard. While organizers were still planning the Columbian Exposition, he read that land value along the Drive was jumping despite a question of ownership. So he decided to buy lots in the path of the boulevard—not from the owners but from the federal government.

His cockeyed reasoning was this: The government owned Lake Michigan. Before Lake Shore Drive had been extended from Lincoln Park, individuals created landfill property between the river mouth and Cedar Street without seeking government permission. The land was worth millions but was tied up in lawsuits. Not having millions to spare, Cox made an offer to buy all this troublesome acreage from the government for $162.42. The federal government, not needing $162.00 at the moment, replied that it had never owned the made land.[7]

King of the Gold Coast

Somewhere in Washington, Nine introduced Streeter and Cox to each other, and they talked over dabbling in a few irregularities; after all, government chicanery was all the rage. Even in Europe it was known that men immune from corruption were hard to find in Washington, and no one seemed to be looking for them.

It appears that Nine told Streeter that he could sell more lots if he obtained something more legal looking to "prove" title. He might have mentioned that one kind of patent looks like another. One of the three went to some sort of government office and came out with a form called a cash patent, and he or a cohort picked up a blank patent application from the land office.

Next, information on the cash patent was copied onto the other form. Nine then seems to have stepped back and let one or the other forge President Grover Cleveland's signature. We know that Streeter carried a satchel of pens and ink for the work. The conspirators might have been emboldened by a tradition that a president is never called to testify.

Actually, Cleveland signed only one patent in his life, and that was for a friend. So Streeter or Cox was imitating the flourish of Cleveland's secretary, Marcia McKean. Between the two of them, they produced an official-looking document stating that the head of the United States government

> do give his [bearer's] heirs the said tract above described, to have and hold forever. In testimony, I, Grover Cleveland, President of the United States of America, have caused these letters to be made patent and the seal of the General Land Office to be hereunto affixed. Given by my hand at the City of Washington on March 19, A.D., 1895. (signed) Grover Cleveland, president; Hoke Smith, Secretary of the Land Office; and S. W. Lamoreaux, recorder in the general Land Office.

No grocer, dry goods clerk or factory mechanic could be blamed for being taken in by this. But a careful lawyer would learn that the patent said to be duly recorded on page ninety-four of volume 6731 had never been received by the office. More telling was that only Cleveland was identified correctly. Lamoreaux had been made commissioner of the office and was no longer the recorder, and Smith was the secretary of the

70

interior, so he was not the person to sign the patent. In addition, Smith's first name was Oake, not Hoke.

As Streeter and Cox took the train home, they might have imagined that soon they would be lighting Havana cigars with $100 bills. Indeed, the Cap'n later told lumber dealer E.T. Sturtevant that he and his friend had "played a little trick on those fellahs in Washington that it will take them years to get on to."

Attorney Shelton, that crafty agent of the millionaire shore owners, heard about the Cleveland document and needed to examine a copy. He arranged for George Detweiler of Toledo to act as a prospective land buyer. Shelton knew that Streeter might relax his usual caution because he wanted to be in Springfield soon, before the senate voted on a bill hostile to any land developed or improved upon by the Lincoln Park Board.

The derby-wearing Detweiler was a little shady himself, having once been indicted for something in Ohio. He told the Cap'n he might buy some land if he could see the patent. Streeter took him to the safe deposit room at the downtown Northern Trust Bank. A few days later, Detweiler pretended interest in purchasing property for $800 or $900 but hemmed and hawed while Streeter grew impatient.

Needing to prop up whatever support he could arrange in the legislature, the Cap'n let the out-of-towner keep the forged patent until he came back. We can imagine that when Streeter boarded a train for Springfield, it was not to convince the lawmakers of his honesty.

Detweiler would testify that all he did with the patent was keep the fake document in a vault until handing it over to authorities. More than likely he gave it to Shelton as soon as he could, and Shelton laid the groundwork for prosecution by tracing the deception to Cox and Nine as well. Only then did Detweiler act the good citizen and bring the paper to officials.

Perhaps Streeter's efforts in the state capital were worth it, because the legislature failed to restrict landfills. But he returned only to be indicted on fraud charges over the Cleveland document. In late August, he was collared at his South Side home by Officer Gallagher of the U.S. Secret Service on suspicion of trying to skip trial and was jailed for a few days.

The forgery prosecution was the strongest case ever made against Streeter, yet once again nothing came of it. There could be no question that the Cleveland signature was a fake, but the government did not clearly establish who had done what. Streeter, Cox and Nine accused one another while claiming innocence, and Detweiler proved less than credible as the chief witness.[8]

The boldness of the attempted swindle led shore owners to have two men from the U.S. General Land Office conduct the first official survey of the former north marsh since 1821, when Indians still hunted among the weeds.[9] This gave them a sturdier basis for keeping Streeter off their land.

After selling his South Side property, the Cap'n returned to the city's north shore with a large white tent and was surprised to discover that watchmen had been hired to keep him off any land other than the approximate area he had created with the help of nature. In time, he would cobble this anecdote together with other events in his life.

Legend: Two Against One Hundred

One day the Cap'n saw at least one hundred men marching his way in broad daylight. "I protected myself. I allus let the other feller fire first. Then—the way I figure it—I've got the right to fire back. So when they attacked, we let 'em have it—birdshot and plenty of it. They kept comin', and when they got up right clost, then we hit 'em with gun butts and clubs."

Streeter grinned as he continued. "You ought've seen Maria swing an axe. A couple o' varments got too close to her, and she cut 'em up bad. They'd had enough right soon. What was left of 'em turned tail and run. There was 33 of 'em what didn't get up. Some of 'em was drugged away by friends, but I got a dump truck and loaded a dozen of 'em into it. Took 'em to the station down on Chicago avenue and charged 'em with disorderly conduct....Next mornin' they wus all fined...Next day the newspaper reporters told me that the mayor had notified the governor that things'd got bad. A state of anarchy, he called it, and swore that's what we had in the District [Streeterville]. He reckoned he might send someone out to investigate and see if the militia shouldn't be called out. Well, I told the newspaper boys, and they printed it, that if the militia got in my way I'd treat 'em just the same as I treated hoodlums and the cops."

—Adapted from Francis X. Busch, *Casebook of the Curious and True*

You might think the winters would drive them off, but the Streeters needed a continuing presence to support the legality of their claim. The Cap'n and Maria would get up in their tent at dawn if it suited them. Always wanting to appear elegant, Streeter trimmed his beard and washed it with ammonia.

Anyone who wanted to come down and talk with him was welcome. Streeter would also walk downtown to see light plays. He loved popular songs but never cared for vaudeville or "Frenchified drama." Drinking was Maria's only known pastime. There is no mention of their swimming, boating or fishing; for them, God created the lake only to increase their real estate.

Despite the couple's unsightly presence, there seemed no stopping the rise of land values along the Drive. A year after Palmer moved to the marsh, the value increased by 150 percent, and as of 1892, it had shot up to $800 a front foot. Yet Prairie Avenue district homes that had gone for $200,000 before Palmer moved across the river were now selling for only $25,000.[10]

Palmer continued surreptitiously blocking upscale residences near the new boulevard, and it would not be until his death that numerous buildings sprang up just west of the Drive.[11] But Streeter's dumping would continue off and on at least until 1910 without anyone seriously trying to stop it and in disregard of an 1899 federal law against unloading refuse into major bodies of water.

The shore owners found some reason to evict Streeter and Maria from their tent, but they left quietly, so the eviction never made the papers. But he considered this just a temporary setback.

Streeter's was not the only attempt to dupe people into investing in land along the shore. One based on the supposed "McKee scrip" was being worked in Great Britain and Europe. That scam involved bribery in high places to claim the entire lakefront from the Prairie Avenue district to Lincoln Park. But evidently, the quick response by the brand-new McKinley administration in halting the fraud convinced him that the shore belonged to the federal government and not the state. That meant he was above the law as long as the president didn't step in.

CHAPTER 5
INDEPENDENCE DAY

During this latest period away from the shore, Streeter gathered a band of people who bought lots from him and who agreed to form a separate government to protect their claim.

On April 5, 1899, the Streeterville men held a meeting in the downtown hotel room he was now using as an office. They voted that the U.S. Constitution would be that of the District of Lake Michigan, and the U.S. flag would be their flag. Then they went home, having done enough for one day.[1] Streeter likely remained and napped on the couch, as he often did. Since there is no mention of Maria in this period, she may have been staying with Chicago friends or with relatives around Detroit.

The new militancy was the brainchild of William Niles, a man with the dreams of a hero combined with muddle-headedness. All personal information about him is lost to us. To Busch, the young glory seeker was a "loudmouthed, pompous ass." No doubt he was drawn to Streeter by the alternating magnetic polarity of eccentrics.

Niles was a good-looking, slender man with wavy hair fashionably parted in the middle and a full mustache. Considering the Cap'n as a crusader for the common man in this era of romantic "little wars," Niles suggested that they take back the shore by settlement. The ragtag army could then establish a fort around an abandoned transient shack called a boathouse, possibly the one built by Avery. Streeter agreed to play the game but seems to have been merely amused by it.

Nearly three weeks after the lackadaisical secession, the Streeterville citizens got around to choosing officers. The Cap'n declared himself the territorial governor and appointed Niles military governor. Jacob Nine was named district supervisor. Elected to the post of district marshal was one of the better-off followers, E.C. Harter, secretary of a downtown cement company.

Notices of eviction were dropped off at the mansions of A.B. Dick, developer of the mimeograph machine, at 21 Lake Shore Drive; businessman and land speculator John Mason Loomis at 55; Robert Todd Lincoln at 60; liberal minister David Swing at 66; Potter Palmer at 100; Franklin McVeigh, reformer of the laws of New York City, at 103; Mrs. Mahlon Ogden, of one of Chicago's oldest families, at 111; Mrs. Barbara Armour, widow of meatpacker George Armour, at 117; George Armour Capet, of the same family, at 120; A.C. McClurg, of the large McClurg Printing Company, at 125; and Orrin W. Potter, vice-president of the Commerce National Bank, living at 130.

One can imagine butlers, lawyers and civic leaders scratching their heads over what the printed eviction demands meant. Despite the odd-and-even numbering, all the homes were on the western frontage of the Drive, leaving an unobstructed view of the lake. (The addresses were later renumbered to conform to the base lines of Madison and State Streets.)

Copies of the notices were delivered in city hall to police chief Joseph Kipley, chief city attorney Charles Walker and Mayor Carter Harrison II, a son of the assassinated mayor.

Unexpectedly appearing on the disputed land was Maria's son, William Jordan. The young man is known to have been there only twice, both times when Streeter seemed about to make more than pocket money. Streeter liked nearly everybody, but not this opportunist, and he denied him any kind of position.

Having a congenial nature except where Jordan was concerned, the approximately fifty-six-year-old Cap'n let the May 1 eviction deadline pass without bloodshed. But on Thursday, May 4, 1899—Streeterville's independence day—the thirty-eight male residents descended upon the undeveloped land and took possession by placing guards along imaginary boundary lines. A more than seventy-year-old guard for the Newberrys threatened to shoot anyone who laid a hand on him, and the misfit militia took a few steps back.

Three of Streeter's men went to Farwell's mansion near Prairie Avenue to demand the removal of the old watchman. Farwell told the delegation that if they wished the paper to be legal, they would have to put "U.S." in front of the marshal's name. When the leader did so, one of his companions sensed a trick and tore that portion away.

A pine pole was attached to the boathouse, and Streetervillians ran up an American flag. A district justice of the peace of what a newspaper would call a "dump-heap republic" banged a gavel to open the court, and shouts of joy could be heard the length and breadth of the land; that is, for a couple of blocks in each direction. Then a citizen who could read aloud without stuttering called out this declaration of independence:

> *When in the course of human events, it becomes necessary for any body of men to take up arms in defence of their property and legal rights, a cause must exist…And, whereas, cities and states do not grow except by annexation, and as there are no records to show that the city of Chicago or State of Illinois, ever annexed any of the territory east of the United States survey of 1821…all of the 100 or more arrests made by the police of the city of Chicago in the District of Lake Michigan have been unlawful and were made with malicious intent either for hire or personal malice.*

The proof cited that the land did not belong to the city, county or state was that no public body ever levied taxes on people buying deeds from Streeter. Basking in his moment of sunshine, the Cap'n told a reporter that there might come a day when criminals of all classes would seek refuge on the lakefront and that extradition treaties needed to be worked out.

Throughout the day, Streeter's militia put up a stockade buttressed by two-by-fours nailed at angles between the lumpy ground and occasional cross braces. The men reinforced the walls with mounds of dirt tamped against the scantling. Though this made the district resemble a colonial fort, Streeterville had its own baseball diamond. But the ball playing and joshing with reporters masked a growing tension. The rebels knew that the moment the flag unfurled, anything could happen, including beatings at the police station.

Farwell believed a rumor going around that Streeter had gone downtown to buy forty guns but was refused. Fairbank's son, Kellogg, walked over to reason with the Cap'n, and later so did Farwell himself and Eugene Fishburn, president of the Chicago Real Estate Board. Streeter told this display of authority that he would take orders only from the U.S. District Court and made Farwell look at an old map showing that the land had once been under water. This proved nothing.

The impending drama ended in farce, starting when deputy U.S. marshal Peterson retreated over the dividing line between the district of Lake Michigan and the state of Illinois, as rough-looking characters accompanying two district officers flashed badges at him. Patterson hastened downtown to confer with U.S. attorney Solomon Bethea, a scowling man who would later prosecute Chicago's powerful beef trust for restraint of trade and help lead America into the Progressive era. But this morning he took no action.

The police apparently were hoping that Streeter's forces would disintegrate from all the anxious waiting. The sunlight grew dim in the shack covered with a canvas sign reading U.S. COURT HOUSE. Inside were an arc lamp and an improvised table. The judges, officers and deputies of the district were either on guard duty or resting on boards, old bedsprings and the floor. The ersatz courthouse also served as an arsenal with several .22-caliber revolvers and Colt repeating rifles, two new revolvers in leather holsters and an ammunition belt with one hundred rounds.

The flag no doubt was hauled down at dusk, and at night, Streeter had trouble sleeping. So he stayed in a chair outside the courthouse past midnight, and at every sound, he turned to see if the stockade gate was being opened. Young lawyer A.H. Baldwin made him realize that a pitched battle would do no good.

At 12:30 a.m., Streeter left his wooden chair and churlishly put Niles in charge. Then he went to the hotel where he had a couch, and in his absence, District Police Chief Murphy deserted.

Chicago's city hall opened early on May 5 for a conference involving Inspector Max Heidelmeier, police captain John Revere, Acting City Attorney Browning and Farwell's son, who was being consulted as a representative of the real shore owners. John V. Jr. insisted on the utter destruction of the district.

At 10:30 a.m., neighborhood boys cheered a line of more than one hundred marching officers led by Revere and Heidelmeier, while the defenders were fortifying themselves with cold ham, hard-boiled eggs and coffee. When someone reported that the police were arriving, the Cap'n threw himself into the chair by the flagpole and picked up a newspaper to pretend indifference. "As a crisis-facer," the *Chicago Inter-Ocean* reported, "Streeter has no equal."

District guards warned Heidelmeier not to step any closer. With a laugh he knocked down a wooden bar of the gate. "In the name of the people of the City of Chicago," Heidelmeier declared in his thick Bavarian accent as he towered over the seated Streeter, "I command you and your followers to disperse."

"I have nothing to do with the City of Chicago," the Cap'n responded, the newspaper still before him.

"Then, sir, I place you under arrest." Heidelmeier tapped the chair with a billy club for emphasis. To the officers behind him, he instructed: "Place every one of these men under arrest."

With surprising swiftness for a man shaped like a walrus, Heidelmeier grabbed the Cap'n by the collar of his tobacco-streaked green cutaway coat and started him on an assisted run toward a patrol wagon while a score of riot-helmeted policemen scurried after Streeter's chief justice and a dozen other rebels. So it was that the District of Lake Michigan fell into enemy hands without a shot.[2]

Since that would not do for a people's hero, the Cap'n in later years would give a more dramatic account to Busch, only he made the scene his former scow-fortress.

Legend: The Collapse of Streeterville

Heidelmeier, with a couple of men, came to Streeter's castle and attempted to serve some kind of writ. Streeter happened to have a number of men with him. The Streeter force made a show of putting up a fight, and the policemen evaporated. If Streeter is to be believed, he chased Heidelmeier with a shotgun and separated him from his men, took his revolver away and led him back to the shack, which he called the District Court House. Streeter called a jury of his satellites. After a mock trial, or, more properly, the mockery of a trial, in which Streeter acted as prosecutor they found the policeman guilty of treason and sentenced him to hang. Heidelmeier was a big, soft, lumbering dolt, and, according to Streeter, begged for his life. The Cap agreed to pardon him if he would take an oath never to interfere with him again. Heidelmeier took the oath and, Streeter said, kept his word.

—Francis X. Busch, *Casebook of the Curious and the True*

All the prisoners were booked for unlawful assembly, with a maximum fine of $100. Since bail was always set at 10 percent of the possible fine, all the fourteen men needed to be freed until trial was a total of a $140. But so many charges could have been filed that a supporter arrived with $22,000.

That no charges of trespassing or fraud were levied appears to hint at conferences with shore-owner attorneys who at every step appear to have cautioned against making a court test. Streeter and Niles were not even roughed up—this time.

From his cell, Streeter told reporters:

> *Why, that land don't any more belong to the State of Illinois or the City of Chicago than Serry Leone or the British West Indies. I discovered it and organized it into a district, and the papers are all on file in Washington. We're only waiting for an Act of Congress, and it'll be rushed in the next session.*

A few days before, Streeter had maintained that the district treasury held $159,000.00 to support his claim through the courts and erect public buildings. But after he sent out for lunch for himself and the thirteen followers being held in basement cells, the treasury was down to $112.79.

No sooner was the Cap'n released on bail at 4:00 p.m. than he threatened to swear out warrants for everyone behind his arrest, including

Heidelmeier. As he said, "They walked right into my trap." As he spoke, ten policemen stood guard to keep the Streetervillians from returning.

The raid marked a change in thinking on both sides. For one thing, having the respect and support of more than twenty others apparently led the Cap'n to believe he really was a defender of the people. For another, some of the shore owners now regarded him as a threat to social order—like a Haymarket conspirator—rather than just a pesky confidence man.

Farwell issued revolvers to his watchmen in a shack on his vacant land just off Streeterville and assured them that, as carried in the *Tribune*, "any forcible entry by anybody without process of law makes such transgression liable to be shot as a mad dog if they do not on your orders desist from such attempts."[3]

On Monday, Farwell told the police to burn everything. Nine officers and several watchmen stood ready as hired men tore down the stockade and set fire to the fisherman's shack and a district city hall that had never been finished. Kettles, a blanket or two and other remains of the one-day civilization were thrown or kicked into fires, and ash piles extended one thousand feet along Lake Shore Drive.[4]

PART 3
A KINGDOM TUMBLES DOWN

CHAPTER 6

INVASION

While reformers in the first week of 1900 were educating voters about city grafters, the former District of Lake Michigan military governor was selling Lake Shore Drive lots that he did not even pretend to own. William Niles needed to enlarge his base so that he could seize the land by force on the pretext of reclaiming the American flag that the police had taken from the district courthouse in May. But Streeter, still smarting from the "shoot as a mad dog" mandate from Farwell, refrained from any effort to reassert ownership.

On January 8, Niles met supporters in an office at 194 South Clark Street for the purpose of levying a five-dollar tax on themselves. Although he told them the money was needed for a district schoolhouse, sewers and water pipes, he used the money to buy weapons and acquire two small boats.

During a meeting on February 16, one of the men paid cash for five lots; another, Sam Scott, who was black, bought two with cash; and Niles bought about two hundred—on credit. From these sales, Streeter collected seventy dollars, which he declined to turn over. Letting Niles wage war on the State of Illinois was one thing, but trusting him with money was another.

At the time, the Cap'n and Maria evidently were staying in an apartment in the town of Englewood, now a South Side neighborhood. This might have been why Niles and his foolhardy band began organizing the invasion at Sixty-sixth Street and South Princeton Avenue rather than some place closer to the Drive.

On May 25, Niles went to the river mouth and gave the captain of the USS *Michigan* an open letter to President McKinley outlining Streeter's claim and signed by an attorney. This, Niles believed, would place whatever happened under federal jurisdiction.

After dark on the twenty-sixth, Niles held a roll call on undeveloped land in the neighborhood of South Chicago, which had been annexed by the city. Thirty men were expected but only thirteen showed up, all district die-hards such as Sam Scott. With them were several Spanish-American War veterans hired as mercenaries.

The invaders loaded their two boats with detachable masts and bags of beans, meat and canned goods, along with tin washbasins, shovels, axes and more than enough rifles to go around. Everyone carried an ammunition belt.[1]

The tiny armada passed several South Side bridges on its way to the river mouth and the lake. The men reached Superior Street at two o'clock the next morning, and Niles marked off the territory to be taken: a large triangular space on both sides of the Drive at Superior Street. Then they announced their intention with the greatest racket the North Side had ever heard—the staccato of a Gatling gun being cranked from one of the boats.

Patrolman James O'Malley actually wondered whether he should round up the attackers by himself. He ran to the nearest police call box and excitedly said into to the mouthpiece, "They've got a boat, should I pinch it?" Not wanting a dead hero, his superior told him to wait for reinforcements.

In the moonlight, the nearly six-foot Niles trod through the shallow water to the narrow apron of sand behind the seawall, holding not a weapon but this proclamation:

> *We, the property holders of Lake Michigan do declare the District of Lake Michigan to be free and independent of the State of Illinois, the County of Cook, and City of Chicago, and that we will maintain our independence by force of arms to the best of our abilities, and all armed forces except those of the United States military, coming into this district, will do so at their immediate peril.*

A Kingdom Tumbles Down

The invaders shoved a flagstaff into the ground and hoisted an American flag. Then, as the property hopefuls stood guard, the mercenaries dug an earthwork twelve feet square on each side of the Drive, about where the Chicago campus of Northwestern University now stands. These were made into "bombproofs" (pillboxes) with roofs of branches, strips of wood and a covering of rocks. Coffee was brewed over a bonfire as daylight neared and the wind picked up. Tired from hours of digging, the mercenaries likely breakfasted on crackers and bread they had brought with them, and true believers such as Scott stood watch.

Lincoln Park Board secretary George Erby was determined to break up this foolishness. At first light, he swiftly drove down the boulevard, but the aggressors jumped up and caught the reins. The men turned the skittering horse around and hastened it back with a few rounds fired into the air.

This brought park policeman Barney Baer down on them. As he raced his buggy toward the invaders, Niles fired a shot that crippled the horse and splintered the rig. Baer wheeled about and made his staggering animal take him out of range.

Next, Niles whizzed a few bullets past Chicago police detective George Hiott. One went through his coat and struck a fourteen-year-old boy in the knee. Another bystander, John Murphy, tried to buggy through with his daughter, but Niles beat him on the head and shoulders with a rifle butt.

Not even Streeter had endangered spectators. City and park police officials sent a messenger to Governor Tanner, who happened to be in a downtown hotel, but he declined to summon the National Guard.

At city hall, Acting Mayor Walker ordered assistant chief city attorney Collin Fyfe to create a police marine unit on the spot. Fyfe and fifteen officers climbed aboard a chartered steamboat and a fire tug. To simulate cannons they hauled aboard what seems to have been a pair of Lyle guns that were used at the nearby lifesaving station for firing weighted ropes to struggling swimmers. The guns were useless in repelling an attack but could make a frightening roar.

By noon, two invaders gave up and sailed away with the Gatling gun and both landing craft. The remaining squatter-soldiers decided to stand against the six hundred policemen rumored to be lining up a few blocks away.

This was too much for Lincoln Park policeman William Hayes, a sensible man with a dark handlebar mustache and easygoing country ways. He merely swung his "baton" by its leather thong and called out, "Say, fellers, cut it out." Niles and his rebels sensed that this "sparrow cop" was a man of the people like themselves and therefore could be trusted.

Hayes and Niles sat down to talk things over in full view of perhaps fifty people watching from mansions, behind bushes and on the grass. "There's two million of my bob here now," Hayes said, "and they're liable at any minute to jump on you and beat you to death. Surrender to me and you won't be hurt."

Niles stood up, and whatever he told his men made everyone look relieved. The invaders unslung their cartridge belts and started turning in their weapons. But Niles clung to his rifle. Policemen pounced on him, and according to the *Chicago Tribune*, "he was pounded up severely before the detective finally obtained possession of his gun, and three more followers in the general melee received some hard knocks."[2]

The time was about 2:35 p.m. The sea invasion of Chicago had lasted little more than twelve hours.

Police kicked in the fortifications, and judging from the bruises covering Niles's face when he was booked, officers had beaten him in the patrol wagon. Streeter showed up downstairs to cheer up his friends.

Niles and a half dozen other men were kept in the county jail for weeks before a jury acquitted them of assault and lesser offenses.[3] Perhaps the jurors could not forget that the millionaires were leaving Streeter's claim undeveloped, as if admitting they could not prove ownership.

That summer, the Cap'n might have thought he was an entrepreneur at last—until the truth about a surge in sales came out. The *Tribune* disclosed that thirty policemen posing as dupes had bought 110 lots from him, using more than $200,000 in taxpayer money.[4] For all their work, the police failed to file charges, suggesting that once again the shore owners only wanted to discredit Streeter while keeping the property question out of the courts.

Barred from the wasteland once more, Streeter lived in Parlor H of the Tremont Hotel. Enjoying even bad publicity, he hung a sign over his door—GENTS' PARLOR—and said he would adorn his property with a tower that would dwarf Eiffel's in Paris. Another time he said he was "going to build a court house and op'ry house and a club and a lot of dwellin's, b'gum. They can't stop us now."

A friend acting as his secretary put in, "The Cap'n's a daisy. He's got 'em all guessing."

Streeter also claimed he would soon be pulling the rug out from under the North Side alderman, Palmer's son, Honore. "Well, Henry Pammer don't live in the ward that elected him. No, sir. Henry Pammer lives in the Deestrict of Lake Michigan."[5]

The Cap'n approached nearly everything with a sense of humor, such as when he and Niles ran for Congress. They produced an official-looking ballot for the "District of Lake Michigan U.S.A." in the November 6, 1900 presidential election. Streeter was listed on the Republican side of the ballot, and Niles opposed him for "Representative, District of Lake Michigan" under the Democrats. They lost.

Should a prospective buyer ask Streeter why he no longer lived on the land, the Cap'n's answer was that he would be moving back as soon as the question of "criminal jurisdiction" was settled. He urged men and women to get in on the ground floor while lot prices were still within the reach.

If buyers didn't show up at his hotel room, Streeter would seek them out during his strolls. "Ours is the only purely democratic government ever formed on the face of the earth," came his boyish voice. "Ours is ruled by the sovereign of the sand." The few lots he sold extended south from Oak Street to what was then Indiana Street and is now the downtown portion of Grand Avenue. Some buyers sought city permits for homes but were rejected.

This year also saw a major threat to Palmer's vision: a group of North Side businessmen proposed building a giant convention center at the foot of Oak Street to draw business away from New York's Madison Square Garden and exhibition halls in Philadelphia and St. Louis.[6] The shore owners squelched the idea even though it would have meant millions of dollars for the city. But even this late in life, Palmer could not just sit back and enjoy his accomplishments. He became directly involved in such buildings as the DeLuxe Apartments a little west of the Drive.

Streeter stayed quiet until September 21, 1901. Under cover of darkness he led about fifteen followers—including some women and a baby—on foot and in two wagons, as if they were westward pioneers.

The urban settlers brought tents with them, trusting in God and the Cleveland forgery. Some in the party may have been hired as guards. We know that three of the men carried rifles.

Police Captain Revere told the edgy elderly watchman for the Newberry family, Henry Russer, that "as long as they behave themselves, I will not interfere."[7]

The most pathetic settler was muscular Billy McManners, a brooding young blacksmith who never had a home of his own and may not have had a dollar in his pocket. He walked ahead of a covered wagon with his wife and baby inside. The childless Cap'n always treated McManners as a son and presumably was offering him a spot of land for free.

Since the legitimate owners had marked off their land with small fences, Streeter's people took care not to disturb anything as they pounded tent spikes into the virgin ground. Instead of settling again off Superior, the Cap'n stopped his wagon near Pearson Street.[8] This made him the personal enemy of feisty Louisa Healy, widow of the portrait artist. She still lived on the South Side but kept up with happenings on the northern shore.

Streeter and Maria not only resided on the land once again, but they also invited wholesale dumping. Before long, the *Chicago Record-Herald* complained that "its dump heap and stagnant water have been a nuisance…Stench and mosquitoes have been its two steady products."

The tent village of Streeterville now enjoyed the largest population it would have in the Cap'n's lifetime. Picturing a colony of cabins, he and his followers erected some sort of small windmill, maybe his eye-full tower. This was too much for Mrs. Healy, or perhaps it was the pretext she needed. Streeter was ordered to move the windmill, which he did— "by three feet." Mrs. Healy obtained an order for complete evacuation.

At 5:00 p.m. on September 20, Captain Revere crossed the boundary and announced that everyone must vacate the district within six hours or face arrest. Replying from his horse-drawn lumber wagon, the Cap'n declared that street superintendent Doherty be damned, "this is my home, and I am here to stay!"

At about 11:00 p.m., most of the squatters scattered at the arrival of a team of policemen and horse-drawn wagons. Sitting on the tailboard of the McMannerses' covered wagon, the Cap'n tore up his eviction order and declared, "There ain't no law can touch me."

He was taken to county jail for contempt of court, and much of the rubble was hauled to the little city dump at the foot of Randolph Street. When he was freed on bail and sauntered over to his new home—the dump—he assured reporters from the rostrum of a city moving van that "I'll stay here for ten years and never leave this wagon."[9] But in time, he gave up and began working out a more inventive way to seize the land—this time as the police and neighbors watched.

To "meet force with force," he swore in twenty district deputy marshals, or, as he sometimes called them, "private detectives." North Siders may have tingled with excitement as they wondered what Streeter was up to.

Just before dawn on October 5, 1901, he mounted the first of two wagons that had been abandoned at the dump and gave the order to roll, if only in a whisper or a gesture under a dishwater sky. His score of bodyguards were ready to jump out and start slugging. McManners, with his muscles dwarfing his bowler hat, held the reins of his mule-driven covered wagon. Jostled inside as the wagon rolled over the lumpy landfill were his family, a few other squatters, a load of lumber and a bagpipe.

Streeter must have wanted the police to believe he had given up and, like the Mormons of southern Illinois, was striking out for a faraway land. The caravan rattled across the Rush Street Bridge and went to the virtually empty Lincoln Boulevard (North Michigan Avenue). Caught unprepared, police dispatched every available officer with a riot call.

Nearing Superior Street, the Streeterville caravan made a sharp turn to reach the District of Lake Michigan. But the heavy second wagon thumped against a sand hollow, and the overworked mules could not pull it out.

Streeter lashed at his horses as city and park policemen came running. When several officers snatched the bridle, the Cap'n said, "Can't you see we are trying to move on? We ain't across the meandering line yet." He meant the invisible boundary separating the natural shoreline from his claim.

Still stuck, McManners resolved to settle down where fate had placed him. He unscrewed the axle bolts and removed all four wheels so that the covered wagon was now a home of wood and canvas.

When the officers tried to grab the blacksmith, his wife threw her arms around him, and four men had to pull her away. She withdrew, but a moment later she threw back the folds of the entrance and threatened them with a revolver she had removed from a soap crate. One patrolman clutched her arm and another thoughtfully wrapped the baby in a blanket. Beefy but nice-looking McManners forced the men to back away and then laid out a pistol, a shotgun and a knife for easy reach.

Although the Cap'n was covered by police revolvers, the officers let him go as long as he stayed off the disputed land. And so he rumbled on toward Chicago Avenue. When the police lost interest in him, he shouted to his horses and thumped their hides with the straps to make a long, dizzy loop in brazen defiance of the law.

This was what his friends had been waiting for. They hoisted Maria from a hiding place to the top of a guard shanty so that she could watch the excitement. Supposedly one hundred supporters cheered as Streeter made idiots of the police. As soon as he stopped on vacant land off Pearson Street, squatters who had been concealed in the shack and behind trees ran over to him, and one of them yelled, "We did it!"

Leaving Streeter alone for now, Police Captain Pecoy gave McManners one hour to vacate. When the time was up, the officers seized Mrs. McManners. She struggled until exhausted, and only then did her husband climb down from the wagon and surrender. The wheels were reattached, and the prairie schooner was hauled away for a confiscation hearing. But Streeter was allowed to stay.[10]

CHAPTER 7

SHOOTOUT ON LAKE SHORE DRIVE

C hicago is always embarrassed about its good-hearted people. One of them was Alderman Mietwagen, who from time to time made the rounds of North Side police courts. Since Billy McManners could not pay his fine, Mietwagen helped him come up with the rest of the money and gave him a used pair of shoes.[1] He and his family then joined the Cap'n and Maria in their open wagon.

Streeterville at this time had two fixed structures: the shack of guards for the middle-class absentee owners and a white tent for the Streeter bodyguards, who would sit on upturned fruit boxes. On the slope of the tent someone wrote U.S. MARSHALS OFFICE DIST OF LAKE MICHIGAN and then, with an arrow, WHITE HOUSE.

When Streeter could not meet his payroll, his marshals deserted en masse. This ended the last real hope of turning his scrap of landfill into a residential district for ordinary people. Maria's reaction to the guard desertion was to enter a Clark Street basement saloon. When the bartender refused to serve her, she went up the steps, kicked out all the street-level windows and wound up in jail again.[2]

Streeter's troubles continued piling up. The man who had sold him a South Side building for a grocery in return for a few hundred dollars and promises, Arthur Bliss, was now demanding the remaining $4,000. Since anyone could see that the graying squatter did not have that kind of money, Bliss may have been hoping to acquire his land claim.

About ten days after Streeter's guards ditched him, he saw workers putting up a wire fence on Cregier property at Pearson Street, which he was now claiming along with Mrs. Healy's land. The Cap'n angrily chased them off with a shotgun, and when they came back, they were surprised to find him acting cheerfully, perhaps on the advice of Maria or a lawyer.

In reality, Streeter's energy and good humor had left him, and for the only time in his life, he was behaving like a sick cat. He and Maria moved into the abandoned guards' tent, and he personally patrolled his claim with a shotgun. For a time, he was refusing to let any stranger set foot on it.[3]

Like Bliss, longtime alderman Edward Cullerton was interested in exploiting Streeter's claim. The politician's reputation for shiftiness had earned him the nicknames "Smooth Eddy" and "Foxy Ed."[4] After purchasing land from Streeter, this plump dean of the city council—and founder of a respected local political family—hired McManners as his landfill watchman. He paid workers to put a shack together for the family on December 19, 1901, and used his influence to keep city officials from tearing it down as trespassing.[5]

After Streeter watched a stove being carted into the prefabricated pine hut, he left the hard-luck family and went to his tent to smoke a black cigar. He should have been more worried. Until now the shore owners had been acting on their own, but at last they were showing organization.

Chester H. Brush, recorder for the U.S. General Land Office, had recently come to town as a witness in a county grand jury investigation of Streeter's Cleveland document. The evidence was a copy obtained by that wily lawyer for some of the shore owners, Henry N. Cooper. Leaving the grand jury room, Busch told reporters in the corridor that "the abstracts of title this man furnishes his customers are fraudulent," and step by step, he pointed out its mistakes.[6]

At last the millionaire shore owners had a strong basis for civil action and did nothing. But on January 31, 1902, Streeter was indicted for fraud. His friends offered to help him fight arrest, but he went to jail without resistance.

The Cap'n had a few new guards living in a shack near the McManners hut, including William Force, Ed Harter and Henry "Klondike" Hoeldtke. As if conducting an arms race, Attorney Cooper hired three guards of his own: Samuel Protine, George Wahl and John Kirk, a young man from Missouri who still wore a cowboy hat. They shared a wooden shed at Oak Street directly north of the blacksmith's shanty. This was called "Cooper's shack," even though the lawyer paid only occasional visits.

Between the huts was a little more than one-block-long no man's land where Cooper's men practiced with smokeless Mauser pistols. Streeter's three "detectives" became jumpy, and something was bound to happen.

Shortly after 8:00 a.m. on February 6, as the mercury struggled up from seven degrees below zero the day before, one of Cooper's guards fired a shot while erecting another fence on the wasteland. Klondike Hoeldtke stepped out of his shack and ordered them to cease fire. Wahl let go with a few rounds of a Winchester, and Kirk joined him. They may just have just been having some cowboy-style fun. Hoeldtke leaped back into the hut and rolled himself in a blanket.

At the time, McManners and Streeter were talking in the tent with the Cap'n's elderly friend, Mrs. Levona Edwards. Hearing the gunfire, the blacksmith grabbed a revolver, and Streeter took his shotgun. With Mrs. Edwards trying to catch up despite her age and ankle-length dress, the two men sprinted across the barren land until they could get good aim, possibly under the cover of weeds or a hump of landfill. Seeing McManners's muzzle pointed at him, Wahl lowered his gun and ran back to Cooper's shack with Kirk.

Later that day, Alderman Cullerton called together all of Streeter's forces to caution them against hostilities. The alderman may have reminded them that in a few days he would persuade malleable Building Commissioner Kiolbassa to grant him a permit for a hotel right where they were standing. Nothing must put that in jeopardy.

In the spirit of nonviolence, Streeter swore out a complaint against Cooper's guards. When a judge held that no one could prove who had fired first, he must have felt that he should never put faith in the system.

On February 12, 1902, Cullerton made a public announcement about his hotel. Supporting him was the acting mayor, chief city attorney Charles Walker. The news jolted Palmer's group. One explanation for the upset is that Walker and Kiolbassa might not have realized what a hotel would do to the further development of the Gold Coast, particularly one on the wrong side of the Drive.

At the lunch break, someone reached the aggressive acting mayor—it could have been alderman Honore Palmer—and strongly advised him to kill Cullerton's ambitions immediately. Walker returned from his lunch break and issued this directive to Kiolbassa: "I beg to advise you that you should ignore all applications for building permits in said 'so-called District of Lake Michigan,' as such, for the reason that it has no legal existence." He never publicly explained his one-hour turnabout.[7]

Since Cullerton made not the slightest protest over what should have been a bitter disappointment, we may assume that someone offered him generous compensation. Foxy Ed lost all interest in hotel building.

Streeter, not a man who could keep things in perspective, had reason to believe he had been sold out. He shared with his English ancestors a passion for abstractions such as justice while idealizing his own actions. Because he was fighting, he came to believe his cause was just.

A little after 5:00 p.m. that day, Cooper and Officer James O'Malley—the same policeman who had offered to wage a lone stand against Niles's Gatling gun invasion—went to see whether Streeter was planning any trouble over Walker's decision. They saw several men running to warn McManners. The blacksmith and Klondike Hoeldtke quietly moved among the winter-sparse weeds with their guns.

"You got no business here with that policeman!" Streeter shouted from behind Cooper and O'Malley, with his finger near a shotgun trigger. "Now, you get out of here mighty quick. Separate them, Billy!"

McManners and Hoeldtke nudged the men's necks with their rifles. After Cooper offered a faint resistance, Streeter knocked him down. Officer O'Malley made a move, but Hoeldtke warned: "If you put your hand down, I'll kill you on the spot."

When Cooper arrived at the police station to describe what happened, he left vague what an associate, A.C. McNeil, was doing in the area. McNeil may have been hiding somewhere as a witness or to surprise Streeter if there were any shooting. He then made a brief appearance at the station and disappeared from all accounts.

During this lull, Cooper's guards, Protine and Kirk, were visited in their hut by young Johnny Allmandinger, whose family still owned a small portion of shore, and by a relative of his, John Schrickel. According to the police account, Schrickel was outside the Cooper shack when through the darkness he saw McManners, Hoeldtke and a third man (Streeter? Force?) walking or creeping along with weapons. All the men on both sides were bundled up, so identifying them was difficult.

"Here they come!" Schrickel called out.

Seeing men coming from Cooper's shack, Streeter's people flattened themselves and inched forward on elbows and knees through dormant weeds. Kirk and Protine pointed their Mausers at the sound. Schrickle ran to call the police and heard two shots fly over his head.

The fullest account of what happened next comes from Protine:

> *I ran out and saw Klondike and two other men skulking along the fence on Walton Place. They got over the fence and crawled behind a clay bank 300 yards away and just as Kirk stepped out from behind the shanty they began to fire at him. I said to Kirk, "Come back," but he just stood there and watched the shots fired.*

Because, Protine claimed, the young man from Missouri's outlaw country had never seen guns fire without smoke.

This is puzzling because only Protine and Kirk had smokeless guns. Why would he lie unless it was to cover up the reason Kirk was standing in the way of the gunfire?

Protine continued: "'It's smokeless powder they're firing,' Kirk said, and then he fired two shots from his Mauser. Then a bullet struck him in the head, his rifle dropping at my feet." The slug had gone completely through Kirk's skull, and he crumpled unconscious to the ground.

In the highly embellished *Captain Streeter Pioneer*, the Cap'n said he and his two friends had leaped into the weeds for safety after Kirk fired at them for no reason. Never mind that Streeter would tell the police that he had kept in his tent the whole time. Moving about the weeds, he allegedly saw a lawyer and a detective for Cooper lying low. One of them supposedly shot Kirk in the confusion and "sneaked away."

If this was what really happened, the lawyer could not have been Cooper since he was being treated by a police surgeon for bruises that Streeter had given him and then took a train for his home in La Grange. It's true that McNeil might have returned to the district, but it is more likely that Streeter saw Allmandinger and Schrickle. Not recognizing them, he could have imagined they were a lawyer and a detective, a word loosely used for sheriff's deputy or bodyguard.

Within minutes of the shooting, three patrolmen, along with Sergeant Culinane and Captain Revere, were demanding to be let into McManners's barricaded shack. When Culinane kicked at the door, the blacksmith shouted, "You stop that or we'll shoot the life out of you." His wife could be heard repeatedly imploring, "Billy, don't make any more trouble."

Revere promised to protect the family if he gave up. After a pause and some shuffling, the door opened, and the brawny man surrendered. The police found Streeter in his tent with a cigar in his mouth. He let himself be led away but said, "I wasn't there at all" and that the gunfire "sounded like a Fourth of July celebration."

Going through the two shacks and Streeter's tent, police seized three loaded rifles, two muzzleloading shotguns and six revolvers, but only one of them was loaded. None was of the caliber used to shoot Kirk, but that weapon could easily have been thrown away.

At midnight, Captain Revere informed the prisoners in the basement cells that Kirk had just died. Turning sullen, Streeter said, "I have told these people [the shore owners] someone would get hurt if they did not leave me alone."[8]

The McManners's shack and the scene of a deadly shootout in 1902. *Chicago History Museum.*

Streeter guard William Force said in an affidavit before the night was out that he had been standing around Lake Shore Drive when he saw eight men from Cooper's camp fire first. Even Streeter reported seeing only three. Under further police questioning, Force became so fearful of hanging that over the next few weeks he gave two more accounts, both contradictory.

On the grim day after Kirk's death, Force turned on his employer and said at the inquest: "Captain Streeter came into the [McManners] shanty and got a shotgun and then went out. After the shooting, I saw Streeter coming from the direction of the shooting with a rifle under his arms."

On February 28, Streeter, McManners, Hoeldtke and Force were indicted for murder. Whether Streeter had been with the others was irrelevant because witnesses reported he had previously given orders to shoot. Force then gave his third account, this time saying that Streeter's people had ambushed Cooper's men.[9]

Every now and then there are hints at how fully city administrations supported the interests of leading families. After the Cap'n posted bail on the murder charge, likable Inspector Heidelmeier was demoted for not

Inspector Max Heidelmeier was demoted for not favoring speculators developing the Near North Side. At the time, the wealthy lived in stone mansions such as this, one of the seven remaining on North Lake Shore Drive. *Author's collection.*

giving special attention to land speculators and other wealthy citizens. The details were never disclosed, but as he groused to reporters, "There has never been a time that the sign of a real estate agent could be tacked to my window."[10]

As Streeter and his codefendants awaited trial, Potter Palmer died in his castle on the former marsh on March 4, 1902. In effect, Palmer *was* Chicago, having been responsible for the Loop and for creating the city's most beautiful stretch of land. He left his wife $8 million and his Lake Shore Drive property, which would make anyone wealthy several times over.

By coincidence, design or perhaps just the absence of Palmer's guidance, the gradual evolution of the Drive now made way for a rapid metamorphosis. Mansions that once stood in isolation were soon flanked by luxury apartment buildings and seemed examples of what up-and-comers felt was wrong with the older generation.

That June 26, Streeter was convicted of assaulting Cooper but was let off with a warning, and his murder trial began. Watching one venireman after another being dismissed later, he called out: "I don't want no man on this 'ere jury who hasn't heard o' me."[11]

Streeter acted as his own lawyer, as if this were no more than a minor scrape with the law. Since there was a question of whether he had armed his men in defense of his property, Judge Kavanaugh allowed a shift of emphasis from the murder to the legitimacy of Cap'n's landfill. That was why Streeter called Fitz-Simons as a witness on July 9. When the loud-mouthed contractor said from the stand that the Cap'n had threatened to shoot attorney Cooper, Streeter jumped up and Fitz-Simons jumped down, and it took three burly bailiffs to separate them.

After testimony concluded the next day, Streeter asked that all his statements concerning ownership of the land be stricken from the record. He must have been concerned about a perjury charge, but the judge told him, "You brought it on yourself."[12] The Cap'n gasped at one point in the closing arguments, as if suddenly realizing how the circumstances must look to outsiders.

During three days of deliberations, a lawyer not involved in the case tugged at Streeter's sleeve to wake him in a chair and asked, "Will you take $2,000 for your interest in the district?"

"Two million dollars—not a cent less," the Cap'n answered.[13]

A Kingdom Tumbles Down

The jurors filed back into the courtroom, and the foreman announced that they had agreed to acquit Force for turning state's evidence but that they could not decide in the cases of Streeter, McManners and Hoeldtke.

The deadlock coincided with the city's most blustery day, July 17, 1902, when a steady wind was clocked at sixty-eight miles an hour and a gust reached nearly ninety miles.[14] The man opening a trapdoor on the Auditorium Theater roof to read the National Weather Bureau wind gauge had to have his legs held to keep him from blowing away. Whatever the origin of the phrase "Windy City," Chicago surely deserved it that day.

Because the city was hemmed in by the southern suburbs and the Indiana state line, it was growing in the opposite direction so rapidly that its relatively small North Township was being called the Near North Side. This was to distinguish the area from the ordinary shops, bungalows and apartment buildings going up north of Lincoln Park and farther inland. At the same time, private carriages and horse-drawn wagons were also being replaced by automobiles. It was a world Streeter must have had difficulty understanding.

Although still free for now, he did not even try to reoccupy the land, and Mrs. Healy ordered the demolition of the McMannerses' shack. Her lawyer, Arthur B. Wells, mockingly told the hefty men tearing it down on August 12 that "you are the only gentlemen who have been in the 'deestrict' for a long time." Wells may have had in mind the time Streeter had assaulted him with a club the year before.

Reflecting the social change of the Near North Side from its wasteland years, many of the men and women watching the destruction were fashionably dressed. One offered a home for the blacksmith's wife, and another slipped some money into her hand.[15]

Three policemen watched over the land through the night. Sometime before sunup, they heard the sounds of people trying to be quiet and found the Cap'n and two helpers moving furniture back onto Mrs. Healy's property. Streeter reached for a revolver in his pocket, but the officers grabbed him before he could hurt anyone. The new trespassing charge was allowed to lapse since he was not likely to get off on his murder charge a second time.

With no home left and no chance to sell other people's land, the Streeters decided to raise defense money by going into vaudeville.

Capitalizing on curiosity aroused by the shooting, they planned to recount their story in a ten- to fifteen-minute act on the regular bill. But just after signing the contract, Maria was hurt falling off a streetcar. She tried minimizing her injuries because she and the Cap'n did not have money for a hospital.

Former judge J.W.D. Pierce, who must have hit upon hard times, filed Streeter's suit over the land on September 27. In it, the squatter insisted that the area had once been an island of his with a channel wide enough for ships to pass through. He must have meant rowboats. The real purpose of the court action may have been to sway his future jurors, just as Streeter's flag-waving solo act played the week before his second murder trial began on November 13, 1902.

Because of the Cap'n joking with the prosecutor, it must not have seemed like a murder trial at all. Pierce and another defense attorney called eight witnesses to say they did not see Streeter near where Kirk was shot. But their testimony failed to make clear where the Cap'n had been at the time.

The jurors retired for deliberations at 5:00 p.m. on December 2. When they shuffled back at 10:00 a.m. the following day, the court clerk read, "Guilty of manslaughter," not murder. Cap'n remarked that his conviction "only goes to show that when a lot of millionaires get together and get the help of the state, the liberty of man ain't safe."

Judge Chetlain imposed a light sentence on Hoeldtke and an indeterminate one on Streeter and McManners, which could mean prison for the rest of their lives. Rather than being sent immediately to Joliet state penitentiary, Streeter was allowed to remain in Cook County Jail, a short distance from Lake Shore Drive, so he would be near the court for his appeal.[16]

To relieve Maria's loneliness, her niece, Nonnie Hollst, visited her from North Dakota. On February 11, 1903, a few months after the streetcar accident, they went for a walk, possibly to see the Cap'n in jail. No longer able to stand the pain, Maria rested in an old barn on Chicago Avenue and said, "Nora, I'm dying—don't leave me."[17]

The Cap'n was drawn aside in the jail that night and told of Maria's death. No doubt thinking of the wealthy living along the Drive, he muttered, "I hope they're satisfied." He was allowed to attend Maria's funeral Mass at Holy Name Cathedral, not far from where they had lived for years on Fairbank's land.

Streeter's spirit withered after Maria's death. Invited to speak to female inmates and a gathering of middle-class and wealthy women studying jail conditions, he instead sang what his grandmother Marion did as he played in her lap a few months before she died, beginning with: "The wilderness was our abiding place."[18]

When the U.S. Supreme Court declined to consider the murder conviction, the Cap'n had no other recourse.[19] On January 23, 1904, he and a wagonload of other prisoners passed through the sandstone entrance of Joliet prison forty miles southwest of Chicago.

But one day, young black attorney William G. Anderson visited him with an idea: using a little-known 1895 state law that someone convicted of a felony other than murder must receive an automatic parole hearing within a year.[20] A decision could go either way, since Streeter would have had such a hearing if he had not voluntarily remained in jail during his appeal. The Cap'n promised Anderson $30,000—which he did not have—if he could pull it off.[21]

As chance would have it, Streeter could not have hoped for a more impartial judge than Edward F. Dunne, a leading liberal and future mayor. Dunne seems to have considered the Cap'n as nothing more than a common crook, judging from the brevity of the hearing and the curt wording of a ruling releasing him on the technicality on November 14, 1904.[22]

Cheers erupted from about twenty supporters. The Cap'n rose from his chair and shook hands all the way out of the courtroom and into the street. Among the well wishers was Mary Collins. The attractive girl—supposedly fifteen or sixteen but looking nineteen—was clearly out for Streeter's supposed million-dollar claim.

Streeter seems to have abandoned hope of ever taking over the land again and returned to the South Side. But two months after Mrs. Healy's death, he married Miss Collins in South Bend, Indiana, in April 1905. The approximately sixty-three-year-old trickster gave his name to the licensing clerk as "George Wellington."

From their first night, Mary kept a log of lies so that she might win a divorce on grounds of cruelty. On May 22, she wrote: "More threats to kill me." Then the most provocative entry came in the exactly one-month-long journal, that during a quarrel "he tore all my clothing off me."[23] But lawyers must have advised the gold digger that her objective was so blatant no judge would side with her. So she left him without seeking a divorce.

Even without the Cap'n's presence, the stretch of real estate he left behind needed a face and a name, and so it became known as Streeterville.

Also around this time, city officials, including Walker, started looking for ways to expand the narrow residential district formed by Lincoln Boulevard, Astor Street and Lake Shore Drive into a true Gold Coast. The shore could be graced with public beaches that would eventually line the eastern edge of Chicago, outclassing every other city in the Great Lakes region. But there was as yet no legal assurance that this expanse would be protected from the clutter, congestion and pollution of commercialism.

Architect Daniel Burnham appeared before fifty-seven of the city's most influential citizens at the Commercial Club with a general plan for transforming the underused shore from the Indiana state line on the south to suburban Evanston on the north into a region of boulevards, beaches and recreational facilities. As he would say later, "Make no little plans, they have no power to stir men's souls."

The final document would be the famous 1909 Plan of Chicago, which offered the poor the same fresh air and summertime leisure areas then being enjoyed only by the wealthy. Because the rapid conversion of wasteland by private speculators threatened to make the dream impossible, Judge Gibbons and others urged that the Illinois attorney general act quickly to preserve the shore for the public.

Freed of Mary Collins, Streeter stayed in the hotel of his South Bend supporter, J.D. Birdsell, possibly for free. While in the city, he met a lonely divorcée of thirty, Elma Alice Lockwood, and they were married later that year.[24] Plain, ordinary, dumpy Elma believed everything her husband told her, including that "land thieves" were cheating him out of the lakeshore. He also told her that he had initially made his money selling copper and brass objects that he had dredged from the lake. Elma also believed that in his first year on the landfill Streeter received fifty-eight notices of city code violations in a single day. As Streeter would say, "I have been arrested two hundred times, on every charge but adultery!"

He also claimed that when Farwell issued guns to his guards before the Kirk shooting, the prosperous merchant told them not to hesitate in killing him. As Elma would paraphrase in a 1924 suit against the city, Farwell instructed them to remember that "a ten million dollar corporation would stand behind them in the crime," no doubt referring to the published sum of annual "guarantee orders" handled by the Chicago Title & Trust Company.[25]

While in South Bend, Streeter and a hired man worked on an old boat he equipped with a raised plank for a bar. But he ran into money problems and was caught trying to steal family ducks for dinner. Then the *Carrie J* sank in a "tadpole ditch," ending his dream of sailing to Chicago.

Streeter and a helper patching up one of his boats, possibly the *Carrie J*, which never reached the lake. *Captain Streeter Pioneer.*

A few months earlier, Maria's son, William Jordan, had arrived on the former wasteland again and tried selling lots on his own for $1,000 apiece. Streeter may have learned of this and wanted to hurry back to reestablish his claim. Jordan never came back.[26]

The Cap'n and Elma arrived on his patch of raw landfill unannounced sometime in late 1909, when there were no longer any guards to keep them out. They lived in a large automobile of the kind called a "motor truck," which they had either found or stolen.

By now Streeter knew how to play the game with the middle-class shore owners. Deciding that he had not created just 2 acres or even the 40 he had asserted in his murder trials, he now recalled building all 186 acres of the Gold Coast.[27] To prove it, he had surveyor George W. Wilson make an impressive but meaningless map of the District of Lake Michigan, which listed Lake Shore Drive as "District Boulevard" and added three north–south streets—Lake, East Lynn and Trilby—that were never built.[28]

Streeter and Elma strolling downtown. *Chicago History Museum.*

As before, Streeter approached potential buyers with his glad-hand and scatter-shot legal terms. He managed to sell lots to fifty or sixty people at an auction he arranged in his stolen automobile/home/real estate office.[29] Police did not stop him as long as he informed buyers that the deeds could be secured only after a final court ruling on ownership, and the legitimate owners never, ever pursued the issue.

And so things were back to normal, except that the Cap'n had shaved off his beard as a favor to Elma, whose name he fondly shortened to Ma. He kept the mustache.

N.K. Fairbank had passed away in his home near Prairie Avenue on March 27, 1903. A little more than a year later, Fitz-Simons died as a result of a fall down the stairs of his Ashland Boulevard mansion, and Marshall Field—one of the richest men in the world—died in 1906. The *Chicago Daily News* later carried a rumor that Field had left $200,000 to fight Streeter's claim, but there is no mention of the squatter in Field's will.[30]

Farwell, who had risen to vice-president of the Chicago Board of Trade, died at the age of eighty-three in his Lake Forest home in 1909, a good but unbending man. This left the huge and tenacious Chicago Title & Trust Company to coordinate a paper war with Streeter on behalf of the estates of Palmer and other shore owners who had been laid to rest.

Because of the charitable trust, many beneficiaries were institutions. They included St. Luke's Hospital (later Presbyterian–St. Luke's), the great Newberry Library research center, the Home for the Friendless, the Chicago Historical Society (now the Chicago History Museum), Graceland Cemetery Associates, the Legal Aid Society, Children's Memorial Hospital, the Art Institute of Chicago and United Charities of Chicago.[31]

CHAPTER 8

THE FINAL BATTLE

Palmer's vision for the former marsh was now a reality, with the Drive one of the most coveted addresses in America. Rather than people such as the self-disciplined Franklin McVeigh and Robert Todd Lincoln, new residents were sometimes social boors or people like self-destructive National Biscuit Company heir Nathaniel Moore. Social commentator Samuel Wilson said the nouveaux riche need only move to the Drive and "suddenly burst upon society as stars of the first magnitude."[1]

Leading the new order was the city's first multifamily palace, the Marshall Apartments at 23 Lake Shore Drive (now 1100 North Lake Shore Drive). The nine-story building with walls finished in English oak featured an H-shaped floor plan, and each of the nine apartments had a reception hall, a large salon, an octagonal dining room and an *orangerie*—a sea change from "greenhouse."

To reach the top floor, one rose in an *ascenseur* (elevator). Each apartment had quarters for three maids, and a billiard room could double as a library. A butler's room was optional. Every resident had his own fruit and wine closet. Rents went for an unprecedented $4,200 a year. But this provided an unobstructed view of the blue, gray or moonlight-shimmering lake, provided you overlooked Streeter's oatmeal-colored stretch of landfill that had not a single tent or squatter's shack remaining.

From the time the first prospective renters looked inside the Marshall Apartments in 1906, dapper Benjamin Marshall became the most sought-after architect in the city, drafting plans not only for other sumptuous apartment buildings but also, later, for the Drake Hotel, the pride of East Lake Shore Drive.

Gold Coast residents now included a number of families who had sold their outmoded South or West Side mansions to move across the river. The result was block after block of unapproachable buildings with carriageway entrances and uniformed guards. As Chicago newsman Ben Hecht observed, everything was open to a reporter "except heaven and Lake Shore Drive."

Some sort of raucous behavior by a few of Streeter's followers led to his being jailed in 1907 for "wild and riotous conduct." A good guess was that he was serving liquor or engaging in some other activity that would offend Frances Willard, the respected president of the Women's Christian Temperance Union. She surrounded herself with sobriety volumes in her beautiful Evanston home.

Judge Freeman Blake fined him the considerable sum of $150 for behavior more suited to "the Wild West than to the well ordered City of Chicago." Curious about the Cap'n's uncharacteristic acceptance, he asked, "Well, have you nothing to say?"

"Only this," Streeter replied, perhaps his high hat in his hands, "I ain't agreein' with you, judge. Streeterville won't never have a chamber of commerce until it has a cabaret. This is a frontier town and it's got to go through its red-blooded youth. A church and a WCTU branch never growed a town yet. Yuh gotta start with entertainment."[2]

Streeter went back to living on the shore as before, only now he had acquired a bulldog named Spot. With the stakes ever higher, a state inquiry commission conducted a hearing in Chicago on the disputed land. A lawyer for the Birdsell estate spoke of how the South Bend hotel owner had paid $75,000 for what turned out to be a worthless title. That was when Streeter spoke of buying it from another hotel owner in Indiana. "I don't recall his name," he added. Since the committee was only a fact-finding agency, no action was taken.[3]

A few of Streeter's lot buyers formed the Property Owners Association to fight for their claim. Their first and apparently only act was to file a suit to eject every shoreline resident between Oak and Erie Streets. The complaint sought $500,000 in damages, but nothing came of it.

Reporters and their readers had come to love the colorful squatter, and by 1910 the Cap'n was being called the "King of Streeterville."[4] And so that name for the area is older than the "Gold Coast." According to reporter Rick Kogan, who grew up in the area, the nickname came from impish *Chicago Tribune* editor Walter Howey in a 1915 headline, "Gold Coast Burglaries." But since editors are not likely to use a term that has no meaning for readers, it may have already been in common use by then.[5]

Attorney William Anderson had grown impatient for the $30,000 Streeter had promised for freeing him from prison, and so the county agreed to auction off the Cap'n's 2,750 lots of doubtful legitimacy.

On December 19, 1911, a deputy sheriff mounted a soapbox to be seen by nearly five hundred hopefuls jostling one another in the County Building and announced: "The titles to this property are figuratively a thousand to one. Let it be understood that the county does not guarantee a title to the land. But those who want it can have it. Start in now. What am I bid for any lot or block?"

Only six single lots were sold, with the high bid being just over $12. Since the deeds went so cheaply, claims for the rest were sold by the block. When everyone left, the black lawyer signed a receipt for $2,525.[6] Though Anderson was disappointed, the buyers went home thinking themselves potential millionaires.

Learning that the Cap'n was close to penniless, Alderman Cullerton used his connections to secure a building permit so the squatter could have a narrow brick store with living quarters in the back at 313 East Chestnut Street, near Oak Street and the lake. Actually, the empty shore land belonged to Francis Stanley Rickords, who was eager to oust the couple but must not have wanted to go against Cullerton.[7]

Evidently, from the time he set up shop, Streeter never sold another bogus deed. His career as a lying, cheating scallywag was over—not that his neighbors would ever accept him.

Once the winter eased, crews began digging a foundation at Oak Street for a turreted forty-one room "castle" at 1000 Lake Shore Drive. Situated on what had been a block-long parkway, this was the first permanent structure ever built in Streeterville other than the Cap'n's little store and the only home on the Drive to rival Palmer's. Stepping inside

The 1912 McCormick mansion, the first permanent home built in Streeterville.

in March 1912 were Harold McCormick, whose father had invented the modern reaper, and his eccentric but philanthropic wife, Edith, daughter of John D. Rockefeller. Even then, elaborate mansions such as theirs were becoming quaint. Streeter could only watch in wonder from the windows of his shop as luxury apartment buildings were constructed to the left and right of him. Neighbors at 1550 included Victor Lawson, the crusading publisher of the *Chicago Daily News*.

As if not noticing them, Ma continued selling sandwiches, and the Cap'n served soda pop to workmen and people strolling by. But enjoying free meals there was young civil attorney Everett Guy Ballard. He showed up due to his fascination with the contrast of pioneer spirits sharing space with some of the city's wealthiest families.

In June 1913, this imitation Boswell sat down for the first of many long talks with Streeter. Perhaps the Cap'n brought out chairs in good weather so they could go over his life by the calm waters. He intended

112

Streeter as he looked around 1913, rather ordinary but still with a lot of fight in him. *Captain Streeter Pioneer.*

publication costs to be borne by the "Improvement Association of the District of Lake Michigan" but advanced the lawyer thirty-three dollars over several installments. This suggests the state of their respective finances.[8]

Streeter had no interest in telling the truth—why start now?—and Ballard embellished the anecdotes further with his half-digested antiauthoritarian ideas. Except for the believable portrayal of a Michigan boyhood, the original manuscript of *Captain Streeter Pioneer* bore so little relationship to the facts that Streeter went to court to stop the Chicago firm of Goulding and Emory from publishing it.

The suit was dropped, presumably when both sides agreed to work out a compromise. Judging from the published version, Ballard rewrote some passages without attempting to reshape the work. The result is not a novel, not a biography and certainly not an autobiography, although it is told in the first person. For one thing, Ballard repeatedly had the Cap'n calling millionaires "dollar hogs," something he was never recorded as saying and which was out of character, since he envied the rich.

With the outmoded frontierism the Cap'n represented, the world did not beat a path to Goulding and Emory's door. For years, Streeter would sell copies from a stack behind his restaurant counter.

The magic that had sent a stolen motorcar to Streeterville also pushed an old cable car onto the small scrap of land that remained undeveloped because of the Cap'n's claim. He turned the vehicle into living quarters and lent it to his guests at the time, Herman and Nora Hollst, the attractive and strong-minded niece of his late wife, Maria. There is no apparent reason why the Hollsts would come to Chicago from North Dakota unless the socially conscious Nonnie thought Streeter was getting too old to care for himself.

He dressed less colorfully now than in his heyday. He either put away his ringmaster-style coat and tall hat or he simply wore them out. He now

Streeter sitting on a barrel by the cable car he used as a makeshift residence for guests just off Lake Shore Drive. *Chicago History Museum.*

went about in a secondhand jacket a bit too large for him and a common felt hat, looking like just another slender septuagenarian trying to take life easy. Streeter kept another dog, a fox terrier also named Spot, and Maria unofficially adopted a teenager, Annie. The girl would stay with the couple from time to time and then go off on her own. Sometimes she brought her baby.

Soon after boisterous William Hale Thompson was elected mayor in 1915, he cracked down on Sunday liquor sales so that he might appear more honest than he was. Any rational man defying the law would do it on the sly, but Streeter threw a party and handed beer bottles to policemen on the shoreline beat so that they might stay friendly.

Several Sundays later, detective sergeant George Cudmore and two other men in plainclothes posed as customers and asked for drinks. Always a good judge of character, Streeter jabbered away to deflect their suspicion and slid a pistol behind his waistband. Then his eyes turned icy, and he made a grab for Cudmore's bottle. But the sergeant told him, "We've got you now, Captain." Seeing Streeter's hand move toward the revolver, Cudmore shouted, "Stop!"

"Stop nothin,'" the Cap'n spat out and sprang back with gun in hand. All three policemen were wresting the weapon from him when Ma rushed in and took a second revolver from a crude cabinet behind the soda bar. Cudmore leaped at her, and she shot a strip of flesh from his shoulder.

Two officers who had been on standby scurried in, and Cudmore yanked the gun from Ma's hands. All five officers threw Streeter to the floor and kicked him. As soon as they dragged the old man outside, Ma slammed the door shut and screamed that she would kill anyone who tried to enter. But in time she relented.

The Cap'n had not been roughed up enough to go to a hospital. When he was released after a preliminary hearing, he joked, "Hooray, the flag still waves."[9] Ma's assault indictment was allowed to drop, but the Cap'n was fined forty-nine dollars for violating the city's blue laws.[10]

Still not dispirited, when Streeter borrowed money to build a chicken coop for his store he explained that the bricks were needed to construct "a Monte Carlo with Chicago as a suburb." Streeter added that he pitied any building inspector trying to interfere. "When these reactionaries [the

Thompson administration] quit cloggin' the wheels o' progress we'll have a nation out of Streeterville yet."

This was one joke too many. Thompson thought nothing of entertaining newspaper readers with publicity stunts and absurd statements against the king of England, but he hated being mocked. An order came down to get Streeter for good. There is no other explanation for what was about to happen.

On the night of November 14, 1915, the Hollsts were sleeping in the old cable car near the soda pop store when a detective stood in the street and flashed a signal. Police vehicles sped down Chestnut, accompanied by an ambulance because of the expected bloodshed. Observers reported that the policemen didn't say, "You're under arrest," and they didn't hold out a warrant; they just threw open the side door and started shooting.

Beer bottles crashed to the floor as twenty officers barged in under the vengeful direction of the wounded Sergeant Cudmore. The police would allege that the Cap'n had a gun, but none was seen by reporters accompanying them. One of the officers struck Streeter with a revolver, cutting his scalp, and a police bullet slammed into a wall just over Ma's head.

"If you have warrants, serve 'em," Elma said, "but don't shoot!"

The policemen grabbed her arms and ordered her to shut up.

At the first shot, Mrs. Hollst sat up in the converted cable car, and her husband stopped washing his hands outside. Some of the more than a dozen officers staying outside fired into the wooden sides of the vehicle and shattered one of its many windows. When Nonnie was wounded in the hip, her husband cried out to the policemen, "For God's sake, be human!" An officer struck him in the face.

While this was happening, Detective William Freeman supposedly was slightly hurt, to the surprise of both reporters who had witnessed the raid. Freeman did not mention the injury to them or anyone else until after their stories were filed.

The officers pulled the squatter out and further pistol-whipped him, and they struck him again as they were pushing him into the patrol wagon. Ma later said, "I saw what an unmerciful beating that they were giving the old Captain. The blood was streaming down his face and his eyes were closed." She called out to the men, "Please, please don't hit Streeter. Remember, he's an old man."

When the back doors of the blue patrol wagon opened at station, the wounded Mrs. Hollst asked to call a friend, a brother of police chief Charles Healey, but the officers would not let her. Rather than being taken to a hospital, she was kept in the women's cell.

The raiders were now free to take anything that might be useful to the Streeters, from money to documents, and used night sticks to smash everything else—including more than one hundred bottles of beer. The officers finally poured gasoline over Streeter's bed but for some reason declined to set it on fire. Instead, they strolled off with fourteen pies Ma had baked for her customers.

Ballard went to the scene of what he called a "police orgy" and brought a Dr. Ecke to treat Streeter in the men's lockup. By then, blood from the Cap'n's scalp had saturated his shirt. In time, Streeter was released on bail and went home. Ever the mythmaker, he looked over the carnage and told a newsman: "They wanted my papers. They wanted the things that prove the right I have to my property—Indian grants, the government patent rights, my soldier scrip and all. I guess the whole business is in the hands of the Chicago Title & Trust Company by this time."[11]

Then he and Ma played a week of vaudeville at the McVickers Theater downtown.

When Streeter's assault trial came around, he told the jury about his thirty years of fighting the police and added, "I'm not seeking your sympathy. All I want is justice. That's all, I reckon, gentlemen; just justice."[12] Once again, he was acquitted. Beaming, he hugged his wife and said, "I'm some lawyer, ain't I, old woman?"

Although the following day was Thanksgiving, it was a municipal workday, and Streeter showed up in city hall to demand his confiscated weapons. The release order came from city custodian DeWitt Cregier Jr., who had helped bring his wrecked excursion boat to the shore after a storm in 1886. The person reluctantly handing over the guns and ammunition was none other than Sergeant Cudmore. What glares those two men must have exchanged! With the weapons bundled under his arm, Streeter walked out of the den of his enemies in a final triumph.

The Gold Coast continued to reflect the past and the present side by side. The Lincoln Boulevard development at the northern end of Pine Street had not realized its potential with Lake Shore Drive just a few blocks to the east, and so businessmen in 1918 invited architects to plan commercial development immediately north of the river.[13] The result would become North Michigan Avenue—the Magnificent Mile of fashionable shops and awesome structures such as the Wrigley Building and the Tribune Tower.

There was no room for a soda pop store near the Drive. John Allmandinger and heirs of the Robert Kinzie family of Chicago pioneers filed a suit to reclaim the small plot of land where the store was located.[14] As a real gale swept gray waves and foam over the boulevard, Judge Merritt Pinkney ruled on March 9, 1918—long after anyone really cared—that the 1895 Cleveland document was a "clumsy forgery."[15] He might have added that the Streeters therefore had no right to remain there, but he did not.

Where the Streeters lived, then, was actually limbo: the Cap'n had no legal right to the property, and yet no one was forcing him off it.

That changed nine months later. As he was showing two prospective buyers around on December 10, they announced that they really were agents of the Chicago Title & Trust Company. A handful of policemen suddenly materialized from various hiding places. The title men said they were acting at the request of one of the owners, Francis Rickords, who, judging from his unusual last name, was possibly related to an officer of the company. Ma grabbed an axe but was quickly disarmed.

The Cap'n and Ma helplessly watched as workers knocked down the brick walls of their store and backroom home. "The fight ain't begun yet," Streeter said. But later in the day, he puffed on his cigar and told a reporter, "If it wasn't for Ma, mabbe I couldn't have lasted all this time."

Ma said, "Me and the Cap'n's a great pair."

Now homeless, they built a bonfire, sat on the ground and stared at what had been. Streeter had no energy left, and the destruction was final proof that Chicago didn't want him anymore. Once he had been a folk hero, now he was an embarrassment.

The Cap'n put on a fur coat and fashioned a lean-to from an old chest of drawers and other material he picked out of a heap of belongings that had been dumped into the street. A few friends came by to comfort him. One old man used the firelight to recite bad poetry he had just written.

"Come on, you tightwads," said a woman in the group. "Each of you give the Captain a dollar. I'll start it with five."

Streeter took the money—we don't know how much it was—and said, "I'll law 'em out of the last brick of them 'flat' houses," meaning the lofty apartment buildings and cooperatives, which were similar to condominiums of today.[16]

All alone after dawn the next day, the Cap'n and Ma walked off the land, and no one knew where they had gone; no one seemed to care. Someone from the title company attached to the lean-to a hand-lettered cardboard sign reading PRIVATE NO TRESPASSING.

Now there was nothing stopping the total development of Lake Shore Drive. Something about the boulevard inspired people to think of greater things. Back in 1916, Colonel William Nelson Pelouze of the Illinois National Guard, brother-in-law of Mayor Thompson, had erected a factory at the foot of Ohio Street. Not much later, he and other members of the Chicago Plan Commission decided that this went against the spirit of Daniel Burnham's concept of keeping the entire shoreline open for public recreation.

Pelouze turned his fairly new factory into the first office and residential building on the Drive.[17] The owners of other lakeside factories near the river mouth also began converting their land into residences or mixed-use buildings.

Among the later tenants of the Pelouze Building, at 230 East Ohio, was German-born architect Ludwig Mies van der Rohe, who would design a number of buildings still gracing the Gold Coast. Pelouze also joined civic leaders in encouraging the city to take over all the parks and build the Drive all the way from near the northern boundary at least to Jackson Park on the South Side. The seemingly unachievable Burnham Plan was being accomplished through private enterprise rather than civic action.

North Siders had become so used to no longer seeing Streeter living and laughing in defiance of the police and the millionaires that few realized he was still alive. He and Ma had retired to an old houseboat in Indiana Harbor, an East Chicago canal that Inland Steel had built in 1901 in exchange for free land. There the Cap'n maintained a semblance of frontier life, and Ma became accustomed to outdoor living and her husband's talkative ways.

Only one person had not given up the fight. In early September 1920, William Niles notified the American Legion that he would lead another assault upon the Gold Coast. On the sixth, he planted an American flag somewhere on the north lakefront and waited several hours for an army of legionnaires to join him. After not a single person showed up, he went home to sulk.[18]

Streeter intended to change the name of the former army speedboat that was his home from the *Vamoose* to the *Elma* in his wife's honor, but he didn't have the energy to repaint the hull. Friends calling themselves the Lake Michigan Land Association would check on him from time to time, but the visits were becoming sad.

While the Cap'n was chopping wood with an axe, a splinter caught in his right eye, and he treated the injury himself.[19] As a result, he was now blind in that eye. Then in midwinter, he began shaking and coughing with pneumonia. He died aboard the boat on January 21, 1921—in full illusion, just like Don Quixote.

Ma told supporters that just before dying, the Cap'n had asked to be buried in the District of Lake Michigan. But the shore owners would not allow it, and the newspapers declined to publish an appeal. Then, someone unaware that the Cap'n had been a deserter notified the Grand Army of the Republic, a Civil War veterans group that was still politically influential in Chicago.

These men in their seventies and eighties knew from newspaper accounts that the Cap'n had claimed two war wounds and spoke of being in one battle after another, and this was good enough for them. And so the GAR arranged one of the grandest funerals for a common man the city has ever seen.

Streeter supporter Casper Smith somehow found clothes similar to the ones the Cap'n was known for. "I'd worry the rest of my life figuring how the Cap'n would feel if he knew he was buried without the stovepipe and the [Prince] Albert [coat]," Smith said.[20]

The tall hat rested on an American flag draped over Streeter's handsome coffin in the Grace Episcopal Methodist Church near the district. Just in front of the casket was a GAR wreath with a ribbon reading: "At Rest, Our Beloved Member"—not that Streeter had been a member of anything.

Among those filing into the church were Elma and her unofficially adopted daughter, Annie, the Hollsts and an uncounted number of GAR members and their relatives. Looking at the coffin, Lake Michigan Land Association member Bill Blaskie reflected that Streeter "was six armies by himself."

"Somewhere, I don't know where," Blaskie continued, "but somewhere the old boy is fighting yet."

Someone swiped the hat from atop the casket before pallbearers carried it to the gray hearse.

North Side traffic was disrupted as Mayor Thompson, who had ordered the vicious raid on Streeter five years earlier, led a forty-car motorcade of Union army survivors and land association members to the last resting place for many of Chicago's great men, Graceland Cemetery at Clark Street and Irving Park Road.

Streeter's funeral service in 1921. *From left (front row):* Annie, Nonnie Hollst, Elma and Herman Hollst. *Chicago History Museum.*

KING OF THE GOLD COAST

With rain clouds darkening the day, one hundred mourners stood by the open grave. Behind a black veil, Ma was starting to cry. Ballard might not have attended, but attorney William Anderson was paying his last respects. He had reason to dislike the old man but said of the grave, "This is sacred ground."

Someone allegedly spat and said, "He'd rather fight than eat." And then the silvery coffin was lowered into the earth.

The best eulogy came afterward, and from an unlikely source. Chicago Title & Trust president Harrison Riley wrote to a newspaper that:

> *The Cap'n's ideas of law were somewhat at variance with that of the preponderant legal opinion but he was a gallant and able protagonist nevertheless. We shall miss him more than might be imagined. He kept two lawyers and one vice president busy for twenty-one years...may he rest in peace and find his lost 'deestrict' in some fairer land where the courts cease from troubling and title companies are at rest.*[21]

The swindler, legend maker and public entertainer lies at the far northeast corner of the cemetery, and so he and Potter Palmer remain neighbors to this day.

CHAPTER 9

THE WOMAN WITH
A SHOTGUN

The Near North Side was expanding beyond anyone's hope. With great celebration, Mayor Thompson in 1920 opened the North Michigan Avenue Bridge, directly linking the Gold Coast with the downtown business district.

Elma still believed that all of Lake Shore Drive belonged to her. In the spring of 1921, she brought the *Vamoose* from Indiana Harbor to a commercial shoreline indentation she called the Streeterville Slip. This was off Indiana Street (Grand Avenue) near the entrance of Municipal Pier, a 1916 exhibition hall jutting into the lake as envisioned by the Burnham group of architects. There she ran a floating restaurant by herself.

Things were going well enough until something happened that she blamed directly on Mayor Thompson. At 5:00 a.m. on August 31, 1921, the final day of the pier's Pageant of Progress glorification of Chicago's business environment, a city scow came loose in a storm and bumped into the *Vamoose*. As Ma recalled, one of the dockworkers exclaimed, "To Hell with Mrs. Streeter's boat—let it sink."

Ma took this personally, and when a carpenter hired by the city repaired the damage, she refused to sign the work order. Perhaps she wanted an apology. She also was convinced that someone had broken into her boat while she was away, sailed it out of the muddy shallows and let it drift a short distance. After fifteen years of living with the Cap'n's

North Michigan Avenue in the early 1920s before its commercial transformation into the Magnificent Mile." *Author's collection.*

melodramatic paranoia, Ma was sure that the city and the "land pirates" were conspiring against her.[1]

The police harbor detail served her with one notice after another for offenses that might have been shrugged off for anyone else. The police allegedly told her that she had better get used to being arrested unless she let the city burn her boat down. When the weather turned colder and customers stopped coming to the lakefront for lunch, she survived on handouts from her family in Indiana.

That October, she announced that she would erect what a newspaper facetiously called "a modern utopia…calling for a stock issue that would permit spending $5 million on land improvements."[2] There *was* land improvement but not by her. Responses to a North Central Improvement Association questionnaire this same year showed that Gold Coast residents overwhelmingly opposed a city council proposal to restrict new construction back to single-family homes.[3]

On May 26, 1924, Ma filed a suit seeking a record $100 million in damages from 1,500 residents all the way from Lincoln Park to the Chicago River, more land than her husband had ever claimed. The defendants included the Chicago Title & Trust Company; the Lincoln Park Board; the Chicago Dock and Canal Company; and the Fairbank, Ogden, Farwell, Palmer, Healy, Newberry, McCormick and Cuddahy families. The names of the others form a virtual social register of men and women from the city's upper class. One of the Palmer heirs was a princess.

Just five days later, Ma's land speculation bubble burst when the Illinois Securities Commission listed the venture as nothing more than a "blue sky" scheme because her backers had no license to sell stock.[4] Outraged by the way the city and state were treating her and desperate for money, Ma filed a suit against the city for damaging the *Vamoose*. Then, to reestablish her ownership of the Gold Coast, she sat day after day in the lonely houseboat with the Cap'n's old shotgun across her lap.

A socialist lawyer in his late thirties named Parke Longworth came along and persuaded Ma to scale down the size of her claim in the future from 186 acres to just 40 "more or less," and so she now estimated the damages at only $350 million. A circuit court judge dismissed the suit "without prejudice," meaning that she was free to file a related one sometime later, but she never did.

Ma's misfortunes continued to mount. Streeter's long-forgotten gold-digging wife, Mary Collins, had sought a divorce in 1922 from Myles Cannaven, described as "a retired wholesale liquor dealer." That is, he probably was a bootlegger. On December 19, 1924, Cannaven countersued, contending that Mary's marriage to Streeter at age sixteen had been illegal. Reporters asked Ma about this, and she insisted that her own marriage was perfectly legitimate, although a municipal judge sided with Cannaven.

Undeterred, Ma filed a federal suit naming the same residents as the circuit court suit, as well as the museums and charities benefiting from Lake Shore Drive rents. On April 20, 1925, U.S. District Court judge James Wilkerson issued a brief ruling that Ma had no right to any part of Streeterville because she had not been the Cap'n's lawful wife and that her interest in the land ceased when she failed to prosecute her circuit court suit against the Chicago Title & Trust Company and others.

Ma looked older than just forty-nine, and sometimes she would drink a little too much, a habit never mentioned while Streeter was alive. At such times, she would be hauled into the East Chicago Avenue police station. There is a credible anecdote from this time that has been passed on by word of mouth. It is said that after one of Ma's arrests—perhaps the one made the day after the federal ruling—a police matron escorted her into the station courtroom. Several times the court clerk asked whether she could come up with twenty-five dollars' bail. Ma looked helpless, tired and out of hope. Isn't there someone in your family or one of the Cap'n's friends who could come up with the money? asked the clerk. Isn't there something you could sell that would be worth twenty-five dollars? According to this unverified account, Ma thought it over and at last offered to post her entire claim to the Gold Coast.[5]

She stayed for a while on the boat and then moved away. No one knows when. The abandoned *Vamoose* was left to decay until the city burned the remains as a public nuisance in 1928. The simple woman who had once dreamed of glory lived out her remaining years in a rear cottage at 1843

Streeter seems to have his eyes on North Lake Shore Drive in Dennis Downes's 2010 life-size bronze statue of the folk hero. *Author's collection.*

Howe Avenue, earning a few dollars selling handmade aprons.[6] She died a charity case in Cook County Hospital on October 18, 1936, and was buried in Locke Township, Indiana.

Many people in Chicago today—even those in the Gold Coast— believe the Cap'n never really existed. Streeter's larger-than-life tales have lasted longer than the truth because every city needs a colorful character in its past. "Chicago cherishes those who succeed," local historian Perry R. Duis wrote. "It may take its total failures, such as George Wellington Streeter, heap blame upon them, scorn them, and then finally forgive them."[7]

AFTERWORD
A WALK ALONG THE DRIVE

I n the 1980s, developer Martin R. Murphy called the Near North Side "the most remarkable urban private enterprise success story in the United States."[1]

When automobiles replaced carriages, Lake Shore Drive served as the city's first expressway. Starting in the late 1920s, the buildings grew higher and incorporated more offices as a result of a friendly zoning code and corporate finance.[2] As early as 1925, a newspaper said Streeter would not have recognized the area he had left just seven years before. Bootleg gang leader Terry Druggan even bought his way out of county jail so he could go back to an apartment at 999 Lake Shore Drive. The north lakefront—alive with sailboats and motor yachts in the summer— also contributed to Chicago's importance as a convention city.

By the late 1980s, the Near North Side had supplanted the Loop as the city's major shopping district and is now included when people speak of downtown.

The Streeterville Chamber of Commerce defines the boundaries of Streeterville as Oak Street on the north, Lake Michigan to the east, the Chicago River to the south and North Michigan Avenue on the west, although Streeter's claim went to Cedar Street on the north, the meandering line on the west and Grand Avenue on the south.

Without fanfare, sculptor Dennis Downes unveiled his realistic, life-size bronze statue of Streeter at Grand Avenue and McClurg Court

Above: The curve of North Lake Shore Drive from short East Lake Shore Drive. *Author's collection.*

Left: North Lake Shore Drive from the roof of the Drake Hotel, 1960s. *Author's collection.*

A Walk Along the Drive

The Near North Side has merged with the Loop to form Chicago's two-mile downtown.
Author's collection.

Aerial shot of Lake Shore Drive and the Near North Side in the 1950s. *Chicago History Museum.*

in December 2010. The eyes of the expressive likeness seem to be on Lake Shore Drive.

If you stroll along the Drive, you might look at the seven remaining mansions and up at the residential towers adjoining them and try to imagine the lives of those who have lived along the city's most beautiful avenue, or at least attended clubs or partied there. This is just a short list of its buildings and occupants:

- 111 North Lake Shore Drive: The Columbia Yacht Club.
- 179 North Lake Shore Drive: The Drake Towers Apartments.
- 229 North Lake Shore Drive: Living here in the 1930s was attorney Silas Strawn, who saved the city financially during the Great Depression by securing private donations.
- 447 North Lake Shore Drive: The North Pier Apartments, with 505 units. In the 1980s, resident Rose Laws was accused of leading a high-priced prostitution ring.
- 474 North Lake Shore Drive: The sixty-one-story North Pier Apartment Tower, completed in 1990, with 505 apartments. The building has a concrete frame and a curving "curtain wall"

Downtown North Lake Shore Drive as seen from Lake Michigan. The Drake Hotel and Palmolive Building are on the far left. *Chicago History Museum.*

of concrete panels in five colors, cast with a sprinkle of granite chips. One of the tenants is the North Pier Athletic Club.

- 505 North Lake Shore Drive: Lake Point Tower, an enormous black monolith casting its evening shadow on glitzy Navy Pier, which has evolved from an exhibition hall to a tourist playground.
- 600 North Lake Shore Drive: Illinois Center, which has a seventeen-story base and a fifty-eight-story tower.
- What used to be 666 North Lake Shore Drive was the largest single building in the country when it was completed in 1926 as the American Furniture Mart. The address was changed to 680 for superstitious reasons. Later, its name was changed to Lake Shore Place, and it became the headquarters of Playboy Enterprises.

Vertical living on North Lake Shore Drive: Lake Point Tower standing in isolation near the Navy Pier tourist attraction. *Author's collection.*

- At 750 North Lake Shore Drive, developer Arthur Rubloff is said to have donated $5 million for a four-story glazed atrium connecting the American Bar Association offices here with the Northwestern University law school addition.
- 840 North Lake Shore Drive formerly housed both the Illinois and the American Hospital Associations.
- Downstairs at 844 North Lake Shore Drive formerly housed Rick's Café Americain, inspired by the movie *Casablanca*.
- A covered walkway links the twin twenty-six-story luxury apartment buildings 860 and 880 North Lake Shore Drive. The "Glass Houses" were designed by Mies van der Rohe with floor-to-ceiling windows overlooking the lake and the downtown skyline.
- The skeletons of glass towers at 900 and 910 North Lake Shore Drive are made of flat-slab concrete rather than steel.
- 999 North Lake Shore Drive was designed by Benjamin Marshall and Charles Fox as a ten-story cooperative. The red brick walls of the attractive 1912 building are trimmed with limestone. One resident was A.N. Pritzker, founder of the Hyatt Hotel empire.
- Edith Rockefeller McCormick's castlelike mansion at 1000 North Lake Shore Drive was torn down in 1953 for a high-rise apartment building.
- One tenant at 1040 North Lake Shore Drive was Michael Segal, multimillionaire owner of the Near North Insurance Brokerage until being convicted of misusing funds.
- 1100 North Lake Shore Drive, site of the much-admired Marshall Apartments, is now a 1980 structure of reinforced concrete with bronze-tinted windows. About half of the seventy-six spacious condos are two stories tall.
- Following Palmer's vision, each unit at 1130 North Lake Shore Drive occupies a single floor in this 1911 Tudor Revival–style apartment building.
- 1150 North Lake Shore Drive was the home of mob leader Gus Alex until he moved to 1300 North Lake Shore Drive and took up with a former Playboy bunny.
- 1200 and 1212 North Lake Shore Drive are expensive condominium buildings built from 1912 to 1914.
- 1250 and 1254 are among the seven last mansions on North Lake Shore Drive. The massive three- and four-story structures were built in 1891 with stone walls eighteen inches thick.

- 1258 and 1260 North Lake Shore Drive are also among the last mansions. The three-story Venetian Gothic building at 1258 was constructed in 1895 for Arthur Aldis. The Georgian-style brownstone at 1260 was built in 1910 for Warren Rockwell.
- What had been Potter Palmer's castle, at 1350 North Lake Shore Drive, was torn down in 1950 for twin boxy, red brick apartment towers twenty-two stories tall. They are connected by a long matching wall.
- The cooperative apartment building at 1400 North Lake Shore Drive replaced the Touraine Hotel. Residents included *Chicago Sun-Times* publisher Marshall Field IV and the offices of Risk Management Services.
- 1420 North Lake Shore Drive was built in 1928 and later bought by the Chicago Bulls–owning Wirtz family. Tenants included socialite Sugar Rautbord and Illinois Supreme Court justice William Clark.
- A 1926 cooperative at 1430 North Lake Shore Drive served as the homes of ballerina Maria Tallchief Paschen, Sears Roebuck heir Robert Wood and Carson, Pirie & Scott president Neil Ramo.
- Joel Goldblatt of the Goldblatt Brothers discount department stores lived at 1440 North Lake Shore Drive in the late 1960s.
- Among the people who lived in high-rise apartments in the 1400 block of North Lake Shore Drive was U.S. District Court judge Walter J. Cummings, who stopped Far South Side steel companies from further polluting Lake Michigan.
- Tenants at 1448 North Lake Shore Drive included socialite Heather Bilandic, wife of Chicago mayor and, later, Illinois Supreme Court justice Michael Bilandic.
- Residents at 1500 North Lake Shore Drive have been other members of the Marshall Field family, as well as radio talk show host Wally Phillips and McCormick heiress Martha Hunt. A *Chicago* magazine survey considered this the best residential building on the Drive.
- The International College of Surgeons is established in the 1912 former mansion of Edward T. Blair, at 1516 North Lake Shore Drive. A statue of *Hope and Healing* graces the front lawn.

- The stone mansion at 1524 North Lake Shore Drive was built in 1917 for Eleanor Robinson Countiss. Her father was president of the Diamond Match Company.
- The Polish consulate general is housed in a mansion at 1530 North Lake Shore Drive, designed with clean, modern lines by Benjamin Marshall. This and the building at 1524 were preserved by the U.S. Supreme Court under the Chicago landmark preservation law.
- The structure at 209 East Lake Shore Drive, just off Oak Street Beach, opened as a cooperative in 1924. Here lived Prussian-born opera star Claire Dux, as well as Gary Fairchild and his wife, Maureen, both members of the law firm Sidley & Austin. In the late 1980s, Jay Pritzker of the Hyatt Hotel family occupied

The lakeward end of East Lake Shore Drive off Oak Street Beach. *Author's collection.*

The inland end of East Lake Shore Drive: the Drake Hotel, the now residential Palmolive Building and the Hancock Center, near where Streeter and Maria fought policemen and deputies for years. *Author's collection.*

the penthouse. On a lower floor lived choreographer Ruth Page. Syndicated advice columnist Eppie Lauderer, known as Ann Landers, resided there until her death in 2002, when her home sold for $3.7 million.

Many of these buildings are depicted on the Internet and have drawn the admiration of passersby for generations.

The beaches are crammed with people in the summer, and the scenery is especially beautiful after a snowfall. And yet, once upon a time, this was a swampy marsh no one wanted until Chicago's leading citizen had the ridiculous idea of moving there.

ACKNOWLEDGEMENTS

In the days before the *Chicago Tribune* computerized all its articles for public reference, I began my research with the handicap of previous accounts, and so I especially appreciate the help of these people and institutions in finding my way. Peter Deuel, a representative of the Cook County Circuit Courts, found a box of Streeter records that had escaped destruction by falling behind shelves. William Fairbank and his cousin, Helen de Freitas, provided me with personal information about their grandfather, N.K. Fairbank. David R. Tinkham of the Chicago Dock and Canal Trust let me take the company's Streeterville file home, and volunteers at the courts in Genesee County, Michigan, provided information about the Streeter family. In addition, I want to thank The History Press for making an exception. Thanks also to my son-in-law, Jerry Smith, and my wife, Marilyn, for preparing some of the photos.

NOTES

INTRODUCTION

1. General information about the Palmers is from Ross, *Silhouette in Diamonds*. The date the couple moved into the castle is unrecorded.
2. Schroeder, "Issue of the Lakefront."
3. Lewis and Smith, *Chicago*, 324.
4. The source of this quotation is lost. The closest account in a book is Farr's *Chicago*, 122. For evidence that Palmer was behind the plan, see five unpublished biographical sketches about Palmer at the Chicago History Museum, excerpted in a later chapter. *The Encyclopedia of Biography of Illinois*, vol. 1, 138, notes of Palmer that "his energies have been with any movement which promised to result in beautifying Chicago." The *Report of the Submerged and Shore Lands* notes that "there is no apparent necessity for the drive as built…The most charitable view of the transaction [project] can only be that it was consummated in behalf of special interests… Public officials have been negligent." That is, apparently felonious.
5. *Chicago Times*, July 7, 1887; *Chicago Herald*, May 30, 1886 (a copy is in the Harpel scrapbook, vol. 5, 1886) and *Land Owner* (1873). For information about how the marsh was an abandoned city cemetery, see the *Chicago Sun-Times*, July 28, 2003; the *Chicago Tribune*, July 29, 2003; and Busch, *Casebook of the Curious and True*, 21–22.
6. For the financial aspects of the Lincoln Park Board, see Halsey, *Development of Public Recreation*, 98, and the *Chicago Inter-Ocean*, May 24, 1894. Brown gives the board's justification for extending the Drive in his report "Laws, Ordinances and Discourses," 60–61.

7. Bryan, *History of Lincoln Park*, 13, said that almost the entire surface of Lincoln Park had consisted of sand dunes. The Drive inside the park was originally intended to join Sheridan Road, which links Chicago with the northern suburbs, and in some early news accounts it is called "Sheridan Road." But the evidence shows that serving the investors' syndicate took precedence.

8. *Chicago News*, March 19, 1893.

9. Stead, *If Christ Came to Chicago*, 71.

10. Wolper, *Chicago Dock and Canal Trust*, 20.

11. This is from the *Chicago Herald*, May 30, 1886, although Fitz-Simons curiously took credit for the plan. In the article, Fitz-Simons also lied about the value of the Drive to minimize its impact. That a lesser paper like the *Herald* should uncover the development plan for merely an everyday feature suggests how obvious it was at this point and how much pressure must have been imposed to avoid further inquiry. Keating, *Building Chicago*, 51, says "Palmer built more than fifty large homes on Chicago's near north side between 1889 and 1890."

12. Pegg, *Dreams, Money and Ambitions*, 21.

13. This inference is drawn from the number of investors and that some were from out of town.

14. *Bird's Eye Views*, 203. The hotel was at Dearborn and Monroe Streets. The guide lists Goudy and Palmer as members.

15. Cox News Service, "Ranch-Auction," January 24, 2003.

16. De Mare, *GPA Healy*, 223. Plats showed that he owned a lot in Block 1 in 1881 and in Block 2 on November 25, 1882. He bought lots in Block 3 ("Palmer's Addition to Chicago") from 1884 through 1890.

17. Associated Press, "Secret Trusts," April 20, 2001. Also see *Chicago Tribune*, November 29, 1994, and *Chicago Sun-Times*, September 13, 1985. As an example of what they wanted to avoid, see the actions of Edward Cullerton later in the book.

18. Testimony of Florence Hutchinson in a deposition in the suit and countersuit, Cook County District Court, Complaints Exhibit 1, *George Wellington Streeter v. Francis Stanley Rickords*. The evidence of this was that there was no public announcement; that unlike a later measure to develop nearby Lincoln Park Boulevard, there were no public hearings; and the board did not put information about the Drive in its annual reports until January 1, 1893, eleven years after Palmer began developing the shore.

19. Hugo, *Man Who Laughs*, vol. II, ch. 2.

CHAPTER 1

1. See *Chicago Tribune*, February 6, 1886. They made a similar arrangement with Shelton Sturgis on December 7, 1885. That Allmendinger was the last holdout is from the *Chicago Tribune*, February 21, 1894.
2. The voyage of the *Reutan* is in Ballard, *Captain Streeter Pioneer*, ch. 11, and Busch, *Casebook of the Curious and True*, 18–22.
3. Fitz-Simons testified at an 1893 legislative hearing that he intended to buy the land off Oak Street but had not yet purchased it. The only reason that ownership of the land was kept open for eight years would seem to be to avoid his showing a conflict of interest. The Illinois attorney general's office alleged that Fitz-Simons spoke at the board meetings, but proof is lost to us. Fitz-Simons's testimony, *Chicago Tribune*, July 10, 1902.
4. The north part of the marsh had been nicknamed Gregortown, after Fristsche, *Chicago Herald*, May 30, 1886.
5. *Chicago Tribune*, July 10, 1902.
6. Fairbank's letter to the *Chicago Tribune*, May 27, 1900; Ambler, Newspaper Scrapbook, vol. 58; also in Brown, "Shore of Lake Michigan," 29.
7. See the *Chicago Inter-Ocean*, May 8 and December 7, 1894; *Chicago Herald*, November 28, 1894; *Chicago Tribune*, November 28 and 29, 1894; and *Chicago Post*, May 9, 1894.
8. Ambler, Newspaper Scrapbook, vol. 58, 197; *Chicago Tribune*, September 10, 1890. For the fate of abandoned boats, see Braun, *Chicago's North Shore Shipwrecks*, 36.

CHAPTER 2

1. *Chicago Daily News*, January 8, 1902.
2. Regarding Streeter's age, Ballard, in *Captain Streeter Pioneer*, had him born about 1841; the 1860 census for Genesee County gave his first name as Wellington and stated he was eighteen, which would make the year of birth 1842. Other records place it at 1843 and 1844. His age at mustering into the army was listed as eighteen, which would make the birth year 1846. Streeter's maternal relatives appear to have been French Canadian, in that they pronounced their last name "Marieu." Settling in the United States, the family gave it as "Marion," and so

Streeter imagined himself descended from the same stock as Francis Marion, the "Swamp Fox" of the American Revolution. His supposed travels to Texas during the war make little sense and may have been invented to cover up for something else.

3. Streeter's fanciful account of his army adventures is from Ballard, *Captain Streeter Pioneer*; his fistula and desertion are from military records in the National Archives.

4. Streeter's experiences after the army are from Ballard, *Captain Streeter Pioneer*; Busch, *Casebook of the Curious and True*, 17.

5. *Chicago Tribune*, February 12, 1893.

6. Chicago Dock and Canal Trust scrapbook at its Chicago office.

7. The park board actually approved renaming the Drive after him for the stretch from the park to Pearson Street, but "citizens" protested, probably meaning Palmer himself. *Chicago Herald*, November 25, 1893.

8. The enabling act for Lake Shore Drive was approved on June 4, 1889. Illinois General Assembly, *Report of the Submerged and Shore Lands*, vol. 2, 207–08. The next page of the report says construction of Lake Shore Drive reclaimed a total of ninety-three acres of submerged land. More information is from Brown, "Laws, Ordinances and Discourses" 60–61.

9. See note 8 above.

10. *Chicago Daily News*, May 6, 1899; Ambler, Newspaper Scrapbook, vol. 58.

11. For information about courts before the 1903 reform, see *Industrial Chicago*, 671; Masters, *Epic of Chicago*, 244; Lewis and Smith, *Chicago*, 322; *Chicago Evening Post*, March 11, 1897; *Chicago Tribune*, February 15, 1903. For civil matters, see *Chicago Legal News* 33, 239, 525.

12. Mayer and Wade, *Chicago*, 273; the writer is identified as Archer in Abbott, *Sin in the Second City*, 9.

13. Gapp, "Michigan Avenue."

14. *Chicago Inter-Ocean*, February 12, 1892, in the Ambler, Newspaper Scrapbook, vol. 58.

15. Feaehan's real estate is mentioned in Winslow, *Biographical Sketches of Chicagoans*, 736–37, and in the *Chicago Tribune*, November 26, 1899.

16. *Chicago Herald*, June 22 and July 28, 1888; also Ambler, Newspaper Scrapbook, vol. 58 (1886–1892).

17. Ambler, Newspaper Scrapbook, vol. 58, 108. This is not an article but some sort of summary, with sources unknown. Streeter continued trying to have the plat registered for at least two years; see *Chicago News*, January 13, 1894.

18. Mayer and Wade, *Chicago*, 180. See Hoyt, *One Hundred Years of Land Values*, 200–25, for the corresponding drop in land values on the South Side.

Chapter 3

1. *Commercial and Architectural Chicago*, 156.
2. *Chicago Inter-Ocean*, January 23, 1892.
3. *Chicago Tribune*, February 11, 1899.
4. Excerpts from biographical sketches of the Palmer family, at the Chicago History Museum.
5. Information on Palmer's landfill, as well as the "warm and steaming" details of nearby dumping, is from the *Chicago Tribune*, February 11, 1899.
6. Streeter filed the suit as a joke against Fairbank, the city and the Lincoln Park Board and then spoke to a reporter about it, *Chicago Times*, March 2, 1893. Wille, in *Forever Open, Clear and Free*, 58, wrote "the builders did such a sloppy job of filling in the lake [the submerged portion of shoreline] that pools of water remained, stagnating and breeding millions of mosquitoes. Disgusted North Side residents finally finished the fill job themselves." But no complaints of "sloppy" work were made in newspaper accounts, critical investigations or later studies. Wille apparently misunderstood the way the landfill was laid, leaving stretches open between cross streets for quite some time.
7. *Chicago News*, May 16 and May 27, 1893; *Chicago Times*, May 14, 1893.
8. The best account of the eviction and its aftermath is the *Chicago Tribune*, February 8 and September 10, 1893. Streeter must have surprised himself with his bravery because all his yarns were variations of this factual incident. Another paper said, "The police were influenced by respect for Mr. Fairbank to such a degree that they refused to protect the Captain's property"; Ambler, Newspaper Scrapbook, vol. 58.
9. The Streeters moved to 7351 South Vincennes, *Chicago Post*, March 13, 1893; *Chicago Herald*, March 14, 1893.
10. Ewing's dismissal of the suit is from the *Chicago Journal*, March 6, 1893, the same day as the ruling.
11. *Chicago Times*, March 2, 1893, and January 13, 1894. See also Ambler, Newspaper Scrapbook, vol. 59, 107. The *Chicago Inter-Ocean* on January 13, 1894, said the Streeters were claiming land from Chicago Avenue to Erie Street and inward for about a block. The deeds were considered

legal only for barter, as a contract between two parties and not for cash, as Streeter was attempting to do.

12. *Chicago Post*, March 13, 1893; *Chicago Herald*, March 14, 1893.

13. *Chicago Times*, May 14, 1893; *Chicago Globe*, September 12, 1893; *Chicago Times*, May 13, 1893. Stockton said the plan, as Goudy explained it to the board, seemed "the best way to get the improvements made"—an absurd statement since there was no reason for the commissioners to be concerned with creating and expanding private property. Fitz-Simons admitted that he owned lakefront land but said he had not yet actually signed the deed. He estimated the value of adjacent Drive property as being no more than $9 million, but May said the value of the "made land" was around $40 million to the city.

14. *Chicago News*, May 19, 1893.

15. The list of secret shore owners is in *Chicago News*, May 13, 1893.

16. Major developments from the hearing are in *Chicago News*, May 16 and 19, 1893; *Chicago Times*, May 27, 1893; *Chicago Globe*, September 12 and 16, 1893. For Sheldon's testimony and "pushing up daisies" remark, see the *Chicago News*, May 19, 1893; *Chicago Times*, May 27, 1893.

17. For the fight between Fitz-Simons and Moloney, see *Chicago Inter-Ocean*, May 8, 1894; *Chicago News*, May 8, 1894; *Chicago Post*, May 9, 1894; Brown, "Shore of Lake Michigan," 18.

CHAPTER 4

1. Busch, *Casebook of the Curious and True*, 44.

2. *Chicago News*, January 13, 1894.

3. Busch, *Casebook of the Curious and True*, 45–46.

4. *Chicago Tribune*, February 21, 1894.

5. *Chicago Inter-Ocean*, April 15, 1894. Newspapers kept poor back files at the time, and none of the reporters seems to have known of his earlier work for Palmer.

6. Casey, *Chicago Medium Rare*, 309–11.

7. Cox, *Greatest Conspiracy*.

8. Details are in the testimony of land office employee John O'Connell in a deposition taken in Washington, D.C., concerning the suit and countersuit, Cook County Circuit Court, Complaints Exhibit 1, *George Wellington Streeter v. Francis Stanley Rickords*. See also Brown, "Shore

of Lake Michigan," 46, about how the forgery was accomplished; Ambler, Newspaper Scrapbook, vol. 58, 107; *Chicago Inter-Ocean*, August 24, 1895; *Chicago Chronicle*, August 23, 1895, in Ambler, Newspaper Scrapbook, vol. 59, 42, in which Cox testifies about helping to forge the document. Details of the fraud charges are in the *Chicago Tribune*, February 1, 1902. Brown at times confused Streeter's claim with the McKee scrip swindlers, who also lost their claim in court. For a bogus claim to the shore land by the Kinzie scrip holders, see the *Chicago Times-Herald*, March 9 and 14, 1897; *Chicago Evening Post*, March 9, 1897; Brown, "Shore of Lake Michigan," 28. Cox claimed he was duped by Streeter: Brown, "Shore of Lake Michigan," 35.

9. This information is also from Cook County Circuit Court, Complaints Exhibit 1, *George Wellington Streeter v. Francis Stanley Rickords*. The survey was made in 1896.

10. Mayer and Wade, *Chicago*, 252. The authors state that "the exodus from the Avenues"—old-money districts such as Prairie Avenue and Ashland Boulevard—"became a stampede after 1893. Mansions on the South Side sold for a fraction of their original cost." The paragraph then describes how these once wealthy areas "slipped into slumdom." Hoyt, *One Hundred Years of Land Values*, 200–25, gives specifics about the decline.

11. Hilliard, "Rent Reasonable."

Chapter 5

1. For the start of Streeterville independence, see the *Chicago Tribune*, January 1, 1902; *Chicago Record-Herald*, May 12, 1909.

2. This raid is the most famous action in Streeterville history. See *Chicago Inter-Ocean*, May 5–10, 1899; *Chicago Daily News*, May 5–6, 1899; *Chicago Tribune*, May 6–8, 1899; *Chicago Evening Post*, March 6, 1899. Details concerning Niles are from his *Brief History*. For a dramatic but fictionalized account, see Broomwell and Church, "Streeterville Saga," 158–59.

3. Farwell's letter and an editorial are in the *Chicago Tribune*, May 8, 1899.

4. *Chicago Inter-Ocean*, May 8–10, 1899. Working from memory, Busch, *Casebook of the Curious and True*, 36, said Niles and others were beaten, but this was a reference to an attack one year later.

CHAPTER 6

1. Arnold A. Dornfeld, a former waterways reporter for the City News Bureau, explained this to the author in the early 1980s.
2. The fullest account of the naval invasion is in the *Chicago Tribune*, May 27–28, 1900. The report states that there were two Gatling guns, but only one was fired. The *Chicago Inter-Ocean* version is too embellished to be reliable. The proclamation is in Niles, *Brief History*.
3. Niles, *Brief History*, 7. The trial is not covered in any other source.
4. *Chicago Tribune*, June 13, 1900.
5. These passages are from a long account of a typical day in Streeter's life at the time, *Chicago Tribune*, September 1–2, 1901.
6. Duis, "The Lakefront," 108; *Chicago Tribune*, September 21, 1901.
7. *Chicago Post*, September 21, 1900.
8. Ibid., September 20–21, 1891; *Chicago Tribune*, September 21, 1901. Mayor Washbourne had established the downtown dump for First Ward street sweepings, and crews built upon it, *Chicago Post*, February 21, 1899.
9. *Chicago Tribune*, October 6 and 10, 1901; *Chicago Daily News*, October 6–7, 1901.
10. *Chicago Tribune*, October 6, 1901.

CHAPTER 7

1. *Chicago Tribune*, October 22, 1901.
2. *Chicago Post*, September 21, 1901.
3. *Chicago Post*, September 20–21, 1901; *Chicago Tribune*, October 6 and 10, 1901.
4. That he was called Foxy Ed is from Wendt and Kogan, *Lords of the Levee*, 40. His building a shack for the McManners family is in *Chicago Tribune*, September 1, 1901.
5. *Chicago Tribune*, December 20, 1901.
6. Testimony before Judge Merritt Pinckney concerning the Cleveland forgery is in Ambler, Newspaper Scrapbook, March 9, 1918. For the trial, see the *Chicago Tribune*, January 8 and February 1, 1902; *Chicago Daily News*, January 31, 1902.
7. See the *Chicago Inter-Ocean*, February 13, 1902.
8. Most of the events from the shooting through the inquest are from the *Chicago Daily News*, February 6, 1902; *Chicago Tribune*, February 12–14,

1902. See also the *Chicago Record-Herald* and the *Chicago American*, both on February 12, 1902; Ballard, *Captain Streeter Pioneer*, 285.

9. Force's third account is in the *Chicago American*, February 28, 1902.

10. *Chicago Tribune*, February 19, 1902.

11. *Chicago Daily News*, June 30, 1902. For details of the trial, see the *Daily News* on July 8 and 11, 1902; *Chicago Tribune*, June 27 and 30, and July 10, 1902 (Fitz-Simons's testimony); the *Chicago American*, July 8–9, 1902; and the *Chicago Inter-Ocean*, July 10, 1902. The *American*'s account added: "No prize for veracity is known to be possessed by any citizen of the District of Lake Michigan."

12. *Chicago Inter-Ocean*, July 10, 1902; *Chicago American*, July 9, 1902.

13. *Chicago Daily News*, July 16, 1902.

14. Ibid., July 17, 1902, and other newspapers. The record as of early 2011 has never been beaten.

15. *Chicago Daily News*, October 22, 1901; *Chicago Tribune*, August 13, 1902.

16. For Streeter's second murder trial, see the *Chicago Tribune*, November 11, 1902; *Chicago Inter-Ocean*, December 4, 1902; *Chicago Daily News*, December 3, 1902. The *Daily News* reported an attempt to sway the jurors in Streeter's favor by sending fake legal documents to one of them, but bailiff Meyer Kaplan intercepted them. If true, this may have been an attempt by one of Streeter's lawyers or backers rather than the Cap'n himself.

17. *Chicago Tribune*, February 12–14, 1903.

18. Ibid., August 27, 1903.

19. The decision was made on January 13, 1904. *Chicago Tribune*, September 19, 1903; January 14, 1904.

20. The law is in the *Chicago Legal News* 36, 268, at the Chicago Bar Association Library.

21. We know the arrangement from a suit Anderson later filed against Streeter: *Chicago Record-Herald*, October 4, 1910.

22. Judge Dunne's decision is covered in the *Chicago Record-Herald*, November 14, 1904; *Chicago Daily News*, November 15, 1904. Some information is in the *Chicago Tribune*, August 15, 1909. From the writing, it appears that Streeter had such a small chance of winning that none of the newspapers had staffed the hearing. A policeman or bailiff may have run about the building alerting reporters so they could reach Streeter while he was still on the grounds.

23. *Chicago Inter-Ocean*, April 22, 1905. Streeter's marriage to Minnie is from Ballard, *Captain Streeter Pioneer*, and Busch, *Casebook of the Curious*

and True, 18. Streeter had been passing Mary off as his wife before the apparent marriage. The newspapers were unaware of her age, which came out when another man fought against alimony payments. Details about Mary are also in the *Chicago Tribune*, same date, and the *Chicago Record-Herald*, June 7, 1905, which carried excerpts of her bogus log. That she was interested only in his money may be inferred from the speed with which she rose from courtroom observer to bride and would-be divorcee. Her interest wasn't because of Streeter's looks. Busch mistakenly calls her Helen Felton. No record of the threatened divorce was found when his next wife, Elma, sued the Chicago Title & Trust Co.

24. In her suit, Elma gave the date of her marriage as May 2, 1905, but Streeter was still living with Mary Collins at the time. The suit is filled with inaccuracies. Streeter would call his final wife "a companion blessed with courage and fightin' blood" (Busch, *Casebook of the Curious and True*, 40), but she was no match for the late Maria.

25. These are the words of Elma's suit against the Chicago Title & Trust Co. and many others. See Hoyt, *One Hundred Years of Land Values*, for a year-by-year total of orders through 1924, when the suit was filed.

26. *Chicago Record-Herald*, September 10, 1909; *Record-Herald*, December 10, 1909; *Record-Herald*, May 12, 1909.

27. *Chicago Record-Herald*, July 28, 1909; *Chicago Tribune*, August 8, 1909; *Chicago Record-Herald*, December 10, 1909. Streeter said that "some joker" had stolen the vehicle and that he and Ma then found it.

28. *Chicago Record-Herald*, December 2, 1911.

29. Ibid., May 12, 1909. The deeds were filed with the county recorder's office despite the ownership question.

30. *Chicago Daily News*, February 25, 1909. Field's will is kept in a vault at the county building.

31. They were disclosed in Elma's 1925 federal suit against the Chicago Title & Trust Co. and many others.

CHAPTER 8

1. Wilson placed the new rich ahead of traditional social evils in *Chicago, Cess-Pools of Infamy*. For information about Nat Moore, see Abbott, *Sin in the Second City*, 211–14.

2. Busch, *Casebook of the Curious and True*, 42–43.

3. *Chicago Tribune*, August 8, 1909; *Chicago Record-Herald*, May 5 and December 10, 1909.

4. *Chicago Inter-Ocean*, July 10, 1910.

5. *Chicago Tribune*, December 5, 1999. For filling in the foot of Ohio Street, see the *Chicago Tribune*, August 3, 1904; *Chicago Record-Herald*, April 3, 1910; Winslow, Chicago History file, vol. 4, 46. For beach conditions in 1913, see *Chicago Tribune*, July 17, 1913.

6. *Chicago Daily News*, December 19, 1911; *Chicago Record-Herald*, which perhaps as a joke placed its account in its financial section, December 20, 1911.

7. That the soda pop store was on Rickords's land is from Ambler, Newspaper Scrapbook, vol. 58, for December 10, 1918, and from Cook County Circuit Court, Complaints Exhibit 1, *George Wellington Streeter v. Francis Stanley Rickords*.

8. Information about how the book came about comes from Streeter's suit to stop publication.

9. The wounding of Sergeant Cudmore is in the *Chicago Daily News*. He said he was shot by "Stella," meaning Elma.

10. *Chicago Tribune*, November 14, 1915.

11. For details of the most violent raid in Streeterville, see the *Chicago Tribune*, November 15, 1915. That more than police overreaction was involved can be seen from the fact that in nearly a year—since December 15, 1914—Thompson had shut down only eight other "saloons" on Sunday. See *Chicago Tribune*, November 13, 1915.

12. Ambler, Newspaper Scrapbook, November 14, 1918.

13. Gapp, "Michigan Avenue."

14. Ambler, Newspaper Scrapbook, November 14, 1918.

15. Ambler scrapbook, March 9, 1918.

16. *Chicago Post*, December 11, 1918. For more on the final eviction, see the *Chicago Herald-Examiner*, same date, and an unattributed and undated article in Ambler, Newspaper Scrapbook, vol. 58.

17. *Chicago Tribune*, October 22, 1922.

18. Niles's waiting for legionnaires is from the *Chicago Daily News* obituary for Streeter on January 24, 1921. That Niles planted an American flag is from a long obituary for Elma Streeter in the *Chicago Tribune*, October 19, 1936.

19. *Chicago Daily News*, January 24, 1921. The *Chicago Herald and Examiner* a short time earlier reported that Streeter had attempted to treat it himself.

20. The fullest account of the funeral arrangements and burial are from the *Chicago Daily News*, January 24–26 and 29, 1921.

21. *Chicago Tribune*, January 25, 1921.

CHAPTER 9

1. Ma's somewhat confused account of damage to the *Vamoose* and the supposed break-in are in a lawsuit she filed in Cook County Circuit Court in 1924. She falsified the year of the incident as being 1923, possibly to avoid having the case thrown out. (The original year was erased, and the later one was put in that space.)

2. *Chicago Tribune*, October 22, 1922. The *Chicago Herald and Examiner* on the same date called her preposterous development plan a "Modern Babylon."

3. *Chicago Tribune*, October 25, 1922. For a plan to expand the Ohio and the Oak Street Beaches—not yet a part of a citywide plan—as major public bathing beaches, see the *Chicago Tribune*, October 17, 1922, and *Chicago Post*, October 19–20, 1922. Most of the shoreline was then privately owned.

4. The state law requiring a license went into effect in 1918.

5. The *Chicago Tribune* on May 27, 1924, called Ma's suit "a record" and gave the number of residents named as defendants as 1,500. Cannaven's countersuit is in the *Tribune*, December 20, 1924, and Judge Wilkerson's decision is in a one-paragraph item in the *Tribune*, April 21, 1925. The ruling is not in the federal records center in Chicago.

6. *South Bend [Indiana] Tribune*, October 19, 1936.

7. Duis, "Hans Balatka's Unfinished Symphony."

AFTERWORD

1. Greater North Michigan Avenue Association news release, November 14, 1984.

2. Westfall, "Home at the Top."

BIBLIOGRAPHY

BOOKS

Abbott, Karen. *Sin in the Second City: Madams, Ministers, Playboys, and the Battle for America's Soul.* New York: Random House, 2009.

Andreas, Alfred T. *History of Chicago from the Earliest Period to the Present Time.* 3 vols. Chicago: Alfred T. Andreas, 1884–86.

Ballard, Everett Guy. *Captain Streeter Pioneer.* Chicago: Goulding and Emery, 1914.

Bigot, Mary. *Life of George P.A. Healy.* Chicago: self-published, 1912.

Bird's Eye Views and Guide to Chicago. Chicago: Rand McNally and Co., 1898.

Blair, Edward T., ed. *A History of the Chicago Club.* Chicago: Herbert S. Stone Co., 1896.

Braun, Mark S., *Chicago's North Shore Shipwrecks, Transportation Trails.* Polo, IL: 1992.

Bryan, I.J., comp. *History of Lincoln Park, Lincoln Park Board of Commissioners.* Chicago: Lincoln Park Board of Commissioners, 1899.

Busch, Francis X. *Casebook of the Curious and True.* New York: Bobbs-Merrill Co., 1957.

Casey, Robert J. *Chicago Medium Rare: When We Were Both Young.* New York: Bobbs Merrill Co., 1952.

Chicago Public Works: A History. Chicago: Rand McNally, 1973.

Commercial and Architectural Chicago. Chicago: G.W. Orear Publishers, 1887.

De Mare, Marie. *GPA Healy, American Artist: An Intimate Chronicle of the Nineteenth Century.* New York: David McKay Co., 1954.

Edgerton, Michael, and Kenneth Heise. *Chicago: Center for Enterprise, an Illustrated History.* 2 vols. Woodland Hills, CA: Windsor Publications, 1982.

The Encyclopedia of Biography of Illinois. 3 vols. Chicago: Century Publishers, 1892.

The Epic of Lake Shore Drive. Chicago: Elmer A. Claar and Co., 1934.

Farr, Finnis. *Chicago: A Personal History of America's Most American City.* New Rochelle, NY: Arlington House, 1973.

Farwell, Abby. *Reminiscences of John V. Farwell by His Elder Daughter.* Chicago: Ralph Fletcher Seymour Publisher, 1928.

Fifty Years on the Civic Front: A Report on the Archives of the Civic Federation. Chicago: Douglas Sutherland Co., 1943.

Goff, John S. *Robert Todd Lincoln: A Man in His Own Right.* Norman: University of Oklahoma Press, 1986.

Grant, Bruce. *Fight for a City: The Story of the Union League Club of Chicago and Its Times, 1880–1955.* New York: Rand McNally and Co., 1955.

Halsey, Elizabeth. *The Development of Public Recreation in Metropolitan Chicago.* Chicago: Chicago Recreation Commission, 1940.

Harrison, Carter, II. *Growing Up With Chicago.* Chicago: Ralph Fletcher Seymour, 1944.

Healy, George P.A. *Reminiscences of a Portrait Painter.* Chicago: A.C. McClurg, 1894.

Horowitz, Helen Lefkowitz. *Culture and the City: Cultural Philanthropy in Chicago from the 1880s to 1917.* Lexington: University Press of Kentucky, 1976.

Hoyt, Homer. *One Hundred Years of Land Values in Chicago.* Chicago: University of Chicago Press, 1933. Reprint, Washington, D.C.: Beard Books, 2000.

Industrial Chicago: Bench & Bar. Vol. 6. Chicago: Goodspeed Publishing Co., 1896.

Johnson, Vilas. *A History of the Commercial Club of Chicago.* Chicago: Commercial Club of Chicago, 1977.

Keating, Ann Durkin. *Building Chicago: Suburban Developers and the Creation of a Divided Metropolis.* Chicago: University of Illinois Press, 2002.

Kirkland, Joseph, and Caroline Kirkland. *The Story of Chicago.* 2 vols. Chicago: Dibble Publishing Co., 1894.

Kogan, Herman, and Rick Kogan. *Yesterday's Chicago.* Miami, FL: E.A. Selmann Publishing Co., 1976.

Lewis, Lloyd, and Justin Smith. *Chicago: The History of Its Reputation.* New York: Harcourt, Brace and Co., 1929.

Lindberg, Richard C. *To Serve and Collect: Chicago Politics and Police Corruption from the Lager Beer Riot to the Summerdale Scandal.* New York: Praeger Publishers, 1991.

Lowe, David. *Lost Chicago.* Boston: Houghton and Mifflin Co., 1978.

Masters, Edgar Lee. *The Epic of Chicago.* Chicago: Henry Raymond Hamilton, Willet Clark and Co., 1932.

Mayer, Harold M., and Richard C. Wade. *Chicago: Growth of a Metropolis.* Chicago: University of Chicago Press, 1969.

McCarthy, Kathleen D. *Noblesse Oblige: Culture and Cultural Philanthropy in Chicago 1849–1929.* Chicago: University of Chicago Press, 1982.

Moran, George E., ed. *Moran's Dictionary of Chicago and Vicinity.* Chicago: George E. Moran Co., 1909.

Moses, J. *History of Chicago.* Vol. 3. Chicago: Munsell and Co., 1895.

Pegg, Betsy. *Dreams, Money and Ambitions: A History of Real Estate in Chicago.* Chicago: Chicago Real Estate Board, 1983.

Pierce, Bessie Louise. *A History of Chicago.* Vol. 3. New York: Alfred A. Knopf, 1957.

A Portfolio of Fine Apartment Homes. Chicago: Baird and Warner, 1928.

Ross, Isabel. *Silhouette in Diamonds: The Life of Mrs. Potter Palmer.* New York: Harper Brothers, 1960.

Stead, William. *If Christ Came to Chicago.* Chicago: Laird and Lee, 1894.

Steiner, Frances H. *The Architecture of Chicago's Loop: A Guide to the Central and Nearby Districts.* Batavia, IL: Sigma Press, 1998.

Wendt, Lloyd, and Herman Kogan. *Lords of the Levee: The Story of Bathhouse John and Hinky Dink.* New York: Bobbs-Merrill Co., 1943.

Wille, Lois. *Forever Open, Clear and Free: The Struggle for Chicago's Lakefront.* Chicago: Henry Regnery Co., 1972.

Wilson, Samuel Poynter. *Chicago, Cess-pools of Infamy.* Chicago: privately printed, ca. 1915. Located at the Chicago History Museum.

Winslow, Charles S. *Biographical Sketches of Chicagoans,* 1948; bound transcript at the Harold Washington Library Center, Chicago.

Wolper, Gregg. *The Chicago Dock and Canal Trust, 1857–1987.* Chicago: The Chicago Dock and Canal Trust, 1988.

ARTICLES, REPORTS AND NEWSPAPER COLLECTIONS

Ambler, J.C. Newspaper Scrapbooks compiled for the Citizens Association of Chicago. Vols. 58–62, Parks and Lakefront. Chicago History Museum.

Angle, Paul. "Free Baths Along the Beach." *Chicago History* (summer 1947).Ayer, Benjamin F. "Lakefront Questions." Paper, Chicago Library Club, May 28, 1888.

Bergstrom, Edward. "Captain Streeter, Squatter." *Traditions* 4, no. 10 (n.d.).

Broomwell, Kenneth F., and Harlow M. Church. "Streeterville Saga." *Journal of the Illinois State Historical Society* 33 (June 1944).

Brown, Edward O. "The Shore of Lake Michigan." Speech, Law Club of the City Club of Chicago, April 25, 1902.

————, comp. "Laws, Ordinances and Discourses Relating to Lincoln Park, Chicago." August 1, 1894. Chicago History Museum.

Chicago Dock and Canal Trust archives. Chicago Dock and Canal Trust offices in Chicago.

Chicago Legal News 33, 35, 36, 37, 49 and 57. Chicago Bar Association library.

Cox, William H. *The Greatest Conspiracy Ever Conceived—Chicago Lake Front Lands.* Chicago: W.E. Johnson, 1908.

————. "Origin of Title to the Lake Front Lands." 3 pages, privately printed, undated.

De Freitas, Helen, *Anecdotes and Descendants of N.K. Fairbank of Chicago.* Privately printed, 1956.

Duis, Perry R. "Hans Balatka's Unfinished Symphony." *Chicago History* (February 1985).

————. "The Lakefront: Chicago's Selling Point." *Chicago History* (Spring and Summer 1988).

Economist, March 18, 1939.

Eddy, Mrs. (Levena Edwards). "My Twenty Year's [*sic*] Experience in the Streeterville, District of Lake Michigan." No publishing information. Chicago History Museum.

860–880 Lake Shore Drive. Brocure published by the Commission on Chicago Historical and Architectural Landmarks, 1977.

Flower, Elliott. "Chicago's Great River-Harbor." *Century Magazine* (February 1902).

Gapp, Paul. "Michigan Avenue: The Promise, the Reality." *Chicago Tribune*, July 15, 1984.

Harpel scrapbooks. Vol. 5. 1886. Chicago History Museum.

Hilliard, Celia. "Rent Reasonable to Right Parties: Gold Coast Apartment Buildings, 1906–1929." *Chicago History* (Summer 1979).

Illinois General Assembly. House of Representatives. *Report of the Submerged and Shore Lands Investigation Committee.* 2 vols. 1911.

Kuhn, Arnold J. "3000 Handwritten History Books." *Chicago History* (October 1956).

Land Owner (January, September and November 1887).

Niles, W.H. *A Brief History and Legal Standing of the District of Lake Michigan.* Chicago: C. Swanberg and Company, c. 1900.

Report to the Mayor and Aldermen of the City of Chicago. Chicago Harbor Commission, 1909.

Robinson's Atlas of the City of Chicago. New York: Robinson Co., 1886.

Rodkin, Dennis. "DealEstate." *Chicago* (February 2001).

Roeder, David H. "Chicago Dock and the Payoffs of Prized Property." *Chicago Enterprise* (November–December 1993).

Schlereth, Thomas J. "Big Money and High Culture: The Commercial Club of Chicago and Charles L. Hutchinson." No publishing information. Chicago History Museum.

Schroeder, Douglas. "The Issue of the Lakefront, an Historical and Critical Survey," ca. 1964. Newsletter No. 5, Chicago Heritage Committee, at the Chicago History Museum

"The Seaport of Chicago, 1837–1962." Port of Chicago, Chicago, 1962.

Sharoff, Robert. "Lake Shore Drive Confidential." *Chicago* (March 1989).

Social Register, 1896. Social Register Association, New York, 1896.

Westfall, Carroll William. "Home at the Top: Domesticating Chicago's Tall Apartment Buildings." *Chicago History* (Spring 1985).

Winslow, Charles S., comp. Chicago History file. Chicago History Museum.

REPORTS, ARCHIVES AND MORE

Chicago Dock and Canal Company historical file. Chicago Dock and Canal Trust, Chicago.

Chicago Dock and Canal Company 1927 annual report. Chicago History Museum.

Chicago Lawyers file. Chicago History Museum.
Chicago Title & Trust Co. file. Chicago History Museum.
Chicago Title & Trust Co. scrapbook. Chicago History Museum.
National Archives, Washington, D.C., reference section, military division.
National Climatic Center Environmental Data Service. Federal Building, Asheville, North Carolina.
Potter Palmer file, ca. 1902. Chicago History Museum.
Rascher insurance map of Chicago 1891–1895. Chicago History Museum.

CORRESPONDENCE

Mrs. Nathan S. Davis III.
William Fairbank.
Illinois Department of Corrections, Springfield.
Illinois Department of Parole and Pardon, Springfield.
Records Vault, Criminal Division. Cook County Circuit Court, Chicago.
Volunteers at the Genesee County Courthouse, Flint, Michigan.

DEPOSITIONS AND LITIGATION

Cook County Circuit Court. Complaints Exhibit 1, Superior Court: *Francis Stanley Rickords v. Florence C. Hutchinson et al.*; *George Wellington Streeter v. Francis Stanley Rickords.*
———. *Elma Streeter v. Chicago Title & Trust Co.* Fee book 287, 48, common law, C. No. 03681, filed October 21, 1925.
———. *Elma Streeter v. City of Chicago.* Fee book 248–526, chancery court, filed November 14, 1924.
———. *George Wellington Streeter v. Guy Everett Ballard.* Depositions, chancery division, fee book 191–554, decree 11-3, 1915.

ABOUT THE AUTHOR

Growing up in Chicago, Wayne Klatt was intrigued by the Streeter legend and awed by the buildings and beaches along Lake Shore Drive. After graduating from the University of Illinois with a communications degree, he worked as a reporter and then editor at the City News Bureau of Chicago/City News Service until its closing in 2005. He won the *Nit & Wit* magazine short fiction award and a Paul Harvey award for radio drama writing. He and Gera-Lind Kolarik wrote the true-crime books *Freed to Kill* and *I Am Cain*, as well as articles for *First Woman* and *Ladies Home Journal*. On his own, he has written articles for the *Chicago Tribune, Catholic Digest, Nostalgia Digest* and *Antiques & Collectibles*, as well as the book *Chicago Journalism: A History*.

Visit us at
www.historypress.net